Praise for *The Power Formula for LinkedIn Success*

"Social networks are evolving into commercial networks—a way to find jobs and conduct work—and thus are an increasingly important channel in people's lives. As Wayne points out in his excellent book, LinkedIn is all about making the right connections, which is why we view it as an invaluable tool for recruiting talent that helps our clients win. Buy at least 396 copies of Wayne's book and share it with all your friends."

—Mark Toth, chief legal officer, Manpower North America

"I know of no one who knows how to use LinkedIn better than Wayne Breitbarth. That he is willing to share his knowledge so clearly and concisely is truly a gift—his gift to anyone who needs to connect for business, for fun, or to find a job."

—Robert Grede, bestselling author of *Naked Marketing* and *The Spur & The Sash*

"I own a small business and have followed Wayne's advice to better utilize LinkedIn. By revising my profile, participating in groups, and more effectively using the advanced search function, I've been able to get connected to key decision-makers and drive traffic to our website. It's been a great business development tool for my company."

—Jeff Carrigan, founder and CMO, Big Shoes Network

"*The Power Formula* greatly simplifies the ability of those of us not in the Facebook generation to make sense of social media and leverage LinkedIn for business success."

—Michael A. Dalton, author of *Simplifying Innovation*

"This book is just like Wayne himself—smart, down-to-earth, and full of good ideas. *The Power Formula for LinkedIn Success* explains how anyone can use LinkedIn to propel business growth. With clear explanations and real-life examples, it's a must-read for anyone who is serious about business development."

—Christina Steder, president, Clear Verve Marketing

"While college students are not strangers to social media, having direction and focus on how to appropriately and professionally use LinkedIn as a tool for researching careers and networking with professionals is essential. Wayne Breitbarth gives great instruction for this tech-savvy yet new-to-the-workforce population."

—Laura F. Kestner, director, Career Services Center, Marquette University

"The combination of Wayne Breitbarth's passion for the power of social networking and his real-world business experience, deep knowledge, mastery of LinkedIn, and skill as a trainer make the *The Power Formula for LinkedIn Success* a real standout. This is the one book to buy if you are serious about getting up to speed fast."

—Frank Martinelli, president, The Center for Public Skills Training

"As someone who has been helping clients use the Web and social media as powerful business tools for fifteen years, I'm embarrassed to admit that I never quite 'got' LinkedIn. It wasn't until some of my public speaking engagements had me on the same program with Wayne that I realized what I was missing. Wayne's real-world experience, commonsense approach, and enthusiastic style have turned roomfuls of attendees—and me—into true believers in the power of LinkedIn. I still help my clients with their Facebook, Twitter, and Foursquare tactics, but for LinkedIn expertise that translates into meaningful results, I send them to see Wayne. If LinkedIn is just a part of your business social media strategy, Wayne's book will be valuable. And if LinkedIn is the only thing you do, it's the only book you need!"

—Tom Snyder, president and CEO, Trivera Interactive, and author of *The Complete Idiot's Mini Guide to Real-time Marketing with Foursquare*

"Wayne's delightful book will help you build competence in understanding LinkedIn, gain confidence in using this important tool, and enable you to take the risk of embracing social media to advance your professional goals. Buy it today!"

—Susan Marshall, president, Executive Advisor LLC, and author of *How to Grow a Backbone*

"A worthwhile business book is one that gets turned into a reference guide to be referred to over and over. Wayne has written such a book. Buy one and you'll be less intimidated about Web 2.0, Sales 2.0, and you'll begin to get measurable results from one social media option—because you'll be linked in!"

—Jeff Koser, author of *Selling to Zebras*

"Wayne Breitbarth unlocks the secrets to successfully using one of the most important business tools in today's arsenal: LinkedIn. *The Power Formula for LinkedIn Success* is a practical tool for anyone looking to significantly improve their career, business, or professional standing. Breitbarth's Power Formula provides a simple and easy-to-use method for increasing visibility through one of today's most popular digital platforms. His down-to-earth writing style combined with loads of LinkedIn insights makes this a must-have book for anyone not wanting to get passed by on today's digital business superhighway."

—Rich Horwath, author of *Deep Dive: The Proven Method for Building Strategy, Focusing Your Resources, and Taking Smart Action*

"If you've asked 'Where's the value of LinkedIn?' or 'Why should I invest the time to use LinkedIn?' then you need to read Wayne's book! His Power Formula provides brilliant insight and guidance on how to get started using the LinkedIn platform to get your arms around the most powerful asset you have—your network of relationships. Whether you are averse to technology, or an executive with little time to spare, Wayne will show you where the value is!"

—Michael Kuhlman, president, 123Smarket.com

COMPLETELY REVISED AND UPDATED 3RD EDITION

The Power Formula for

LinkedIn

Success

Kick-start Your Business, Brand, *and* Job Search

Wayne Breitbarth

GREENLEAF
BOOK GROUP PRESS

Published by Greenleaf Book Group Press
Austin, Texas
www.gbgpress.com

Distributed by Greenleaf Book Group

For ordering information or special discounts for bulk purchases, please contact Greenleaf Book Group at PO Box 91869, Austin, TX 78709, 512.891.6100.

Design and composition by Greenleaf Book Group and Publications Development Company
Cover design by Greenleaf Book Group

Publisher's Cataloging-in-Publication Data
Breitbarth, Wayne.
  The power formula for LinkedIn success : kick-start your business, brand, and job search / Wayne Breitbarth—3rd ed.
   p. ; cm.
  ISBN: 978-1-62634-238-5

  1. LinkedIn (Electronic resource) 2. Online social networks. 3. Business networks—Computer network resources. 4. Branding (Marketing)—Computer network resources. 5. Job hunting—Computer network resources. 6. Success in business. I. Title.
HD30.37 B74 2011
658.054678   2012950188

Part of the Tree Neutral® program, which offsets the number of trees consumed in the production and printing of this book by taking proactive steps, such as planting trees in direct proportion to the number of trees used: www.treeneutral.com

Printed in the United States of America on acid-free paper   TreeNeutral®

15 16 17 18 19 20   10 9 8 7 6 5 4 3 2 1

Third Edition

Contents

Bonus Online Resources

The Definitive Worksheet to Optimize Your
LinkedIn Profile Headline
www.powerformula.net/free

The LinkedIn Connection Conundrum: Who Should
Be in Your Network?
www.powerformula.net/connections

10 LinkedIn Mistakes Companies Make—and How to Fix
Them Before They Damage Your Company's Reputation
www.powerformula.net/mistakes

How to Reach Your LinkedIn Audience
www.powerformula.net/audience

How Does Your LinkedIn Marketing Strategy Measure Up?
www.powerformula.net/marketing

Should You Hide Your LinkedIn Connections?
www.powerformula.net/hideconnections

About This Book

This book is meant to help you quickly, efficiently, and pain-lessly discover whether this thing called LinkedIn is worth your time and effort and to understand how to effectively use it to accomplish your business goals. You may choose to read it cover to cover or immediately begin applying the techniques and strategies discussed in each chapter. In either case, it will be an important reference as you move from novice to experienced user. I sincerely hope you will find this book to be motivational, educational, and entertaining.

Also provided in this book are links to a variety of valuable resources to further assist you in using LinkedIn to successfully brand and market yourself and your business.

As with most Internet-based resources, there will be periodic updates and other changes to the LinkedIn website. In order for this book to remain relevant and accurate, I will periodically address these modifications. Visit my website at www.powerformula.net, and sign up to receive these important notifications and/or register to receive free weekly LinkedIn tips.

Introduction

I Never Even Wanted to Be on LinkedIn!

I never wanted to be on LinkedIn, never thought it would be useful, and surely never wanted to spend a significant amount of time teaching other business executives how to use it. I am not someone who loves technology for technology's sake; I am an experienced businessperson who respects the experience and knowledge of other businesspeople. Business professionals tend to be interested in thoroughly exploring the "why" before launching into the "how to." Thus, this book is designed to not only teach you how to effectively use LinkedIn but also to show you why the tools, techniques, and strategies presented here can be instrumental in furthering your professional goals. With that in mind, let me share with you some background on my LinkedIn journey and explain why I think LinkedIn is an important tool for you to investigate and master.

Think back to the time you received your very first e-mail. If you were like me, you looked at that e-mail and said, "Nah, this will never work. People will never communicate this way, and

I'm sure if I ignore this, it will just go away." Well, do you know anyone today who doesn't have an e-mail account? Can you even imagine going a day (or perhaps even a couple of hours) without checking your e-mail?

In my opinion, the whole social media phenomenon, and LinkedIn in particular, has that same kind of feel to it. Although I am not a futurist, it's clear that the process of connecting with people over the Internet is here to stay. When people attend my training classes, especially people in my age group (as of this writing, I am fifty-seven years old), many of them hope the ninety minutes they spend will confirm their suspicion that this tool is worthless or avoidable. It may be your secret desire (or maybe your not-so-secret desire) that when you finish this book, you'll be able to confidently say, "Great. No value there. Now I can move on. My life is too busy for LinkedIn anyway!"

That is why I approach my training classes as well as this book with the intention of not necessarily teaching you every specific technique of using LinkedIn but instead showing you its capabilities so that you can get rid of the fear factor. I suspect that fear comes from two sources: Potential users ask themselves, "What will happen if I jump into the murky waters of LinkedIn?" or, more importantly, "Will I be at a competitive disadvantage if my competitors embrace this technology while I sit on the fence?"

My goal is for you to end up in one of three camps after reading this book. First, you may gain an understanding of the concept and recognize what you might be missing but choose instead to spend your time finding another way to brand or market yourself and your business. That's fine. LinkedIn isn't necessarily for everyone. Second, once you have a better understanding of the capabilities of LinkedIn, you may decide to either tinker with it on a limited basis or strategize about how you may be able to use it to advance your career or business in a few key ways. Or, third, you may decide this is a rockin' tool and realize you'd better get on board completely—and also have people in your company fully understand its concepts, premises, and working parts.

LinkedIn is all about using the Internet to find and be found by people—in addition to using the good old-fashioned face-to-face method of meeting people. Perhaps over time more personal contact will be replaced with virtual interactions, but LinkedIn will never completely take the place of meeting people in your business sphere and spending time with them, either on the phone or in person. People still prefer to do business with people they know and trust, and typically knowing and trusting takes place much more rapidly when contact occurs on a face-to-face basis.

None of us is looking for another thing to do for two or three hours each week to replace spending time with our families, playing golf, fishing, or engaging in other hobbies we enjoy. Therefore, my hope is that the time you spend on LinkedIn will not necessarily add a burden to your already busy life but that it will allow you to do a form of networking 24/7, perhaps while watching your favorite TV shows or sporting events. Being a Wisconsinite, it is my duty to watch the Green Bay Packers play football on TV each Sunday afternoon. However, I have within me this nagging little voice that says, *Wayne, this is not a very productive endeavor,* especially when the Packers are getting annihilated. Now, with the help of my laptop, tablet, or smartphone, LinkedIn allows me to keep track of what is going on in my network of professionals, while at the same time keeping an eye on the Packers game.

LinkedIn is the world's largest online business networking site. You join LinkedIn either by going to LinkedIn.com and setting up an account or by accepting an invitation from someone who has suggested you sign up. Most people are invited by several friends or business associates before making the decision to join LinkedIn, and it usually takes an invitation from a very trusted friend before they get started. However, even after they take the first step, it's common for people to not really know what or why they are joining; they simply check the box and begin the journey without either knowing what LinkedIn does or having a strategy for how to use it.

By the time this book hits the shelves, LinkedIn will have around 400 million users, with two new members being added every second of the day. Approximately 40 percent of those members are in the United States. The following chart enumerates some interesting statistics relating to the demographics of LinkedIn users:

THE LINKEDIN PROFESSIONAL AT A GLANCE

Over age 34	56%
Male/Female	56% / 44%
College Grad/Post Grad	84%
Drive Business Decisions	76%
Senior-level Executive (Director and above)	25%
Household Income $100K+	38%

Source: LinkedIn.com (October 2014); Quantcast.com (October 2014)

Here's how I got started on LinkedIn. I have a very close friend who nagged me Sunday after Sunday at church, explaining that I should get on LinkedIn, and I consistently blew him off, saying, "I don't have time to keep track of your LinkedIn or Plaxo or Facebook or any other website." Yet he consistently said to me, "Listen—you are a small business owner and you really need this."

Well, as luck would have it, one afternoon I found myself stuck in a hotel room in a remote location with nothing to do. It's not my style to spend the afternoon watching TV, so I thought I would check out this LinkedIn thing and see what it was about. Two hours later, I had overcome my fear and ordered two books about LinkedIn from Amazon.com. I now saw LinkedIn as a powerful tool and wanted to become an expert as soon as humanly possible. Four or five hours later, in that same hotel room, I was en route to becoming a passionate proponent of virtual networking. I immediately began connecting with people from my past, including college classmates and employees of many of the companies I had worked with in the Milwaukee area over the past thirty years.

In response to my newfound enthusiasm, friends and colleagues began asking me questions about LinkedIn. After admitting I had become a LinkedIn junkie, I would invite them into our company's boardroom (I owned an office furniture dealership at the time) and spend time sharing what I knew about LinkedIn with them. This turned into a formal class, followed by requests from local chambers of commerce, Rotary clubs, etc. to educate their members about the far-reaching benefits of LinkedIn. And as they say, the rest is history. More than 60,000 people have read the first and second editions of this book, and you are reading the third edition. I am now a nationally recognized speaker, and I consult with companies across the country, helping them use LinkedIn to promote their products and services and increase their revenue.

Despite the fact that LinkedIn is often referred to as "Facebook for businesspeople," what businesspeople appreciate and respect about LinkedIn is that it has significant processes and controls that keep it from becoming like Facebook. At the time of this writing, Facebook has over a billion members, and the ability to connect with such a vast number of people certainly does attract some businesspeople. However, many facets of Facebook—such as pictures of your past tagged with your name (and possibly including beer bongs and bikinis), relationship statuses, and religious and political views—are things that totally turn off most businesspeople to using the site for professional networking. Facebook does have applications for businesses (especially those that sell directly to consumers), but many businesspeople feel more comfortable with LinkedIn because of its built-in controls and personal settings. I will discuss many of those controls and settings in subsequent chapters of this book.

By now you are, no doubt, anxious to get started. So fasten your seatbelt and prepare to see your fear subside as you learn more about what LinkedIn is and how it can help you kick-start your business, brand, and job search.

CHAPTER 1

A New Way to
Look at Social Media

The LinkedIn Power Formula

I had been on LinkedIn for just over a year and had taught more than 120 classes, with over four thousand participants, when I had a revelation: All of these social media tools are just that—tools! No different than a hammer, which is only as good as the person swinging it. As I started to think about this more and more, I realized that there is one group of people—we will call them the Facebook generation—and then there are the rest of us, the non-Facebook generations. The first group is darned good at social media and grasp it so much more easily than we do, since they grew up with the Internet. They embrace new social technologies in a big hurry, which scares the heck out of many of us in the non-Facebook group. So, instead of deciding we should get on board, we just hope it will go away, thinking that maybe we'll wake up one day, it will all be gone, and things will be back to "normal."

I'm not telling you this because I want to bring you down even further but because I have some good news about the person swinging the hammer: you. You already have lots of experience and relationships that you can leverage to make your use of LinkedIn—or any other social media site—much more effective. It is this revelation that helped me come up with the idea of the Power Formula:

Your Unique Experience + Your Unique Relationships + The Tool (in this case, LinkedIn) = The Power

Anyone with business experience and the willingness to learn can realize great benefits from LinkedIn. And getting started with LinkedIn is really not that big of a deal. You can either read a book about how to use LinkedIn, attend a seminar, consult an expert you trust, or check out the Help Center on LinkedIn.com. Learn as much as you can, and then take the time to execute the strategies you have been shown. Make the commitment to get this done, and make it a priority to establish some good LinkedIn habits. No matter how tech-savvy they are, members of the Facebook generation cannot go to a two-hour seminar and come away with the wealth of experience and relationships that comes from years of meetings, handshakes, small talk, weekend retreats, planning sessions, bad proposals, good proposals, winning jobs, losing jobs, etc. But members of the non-Facebook generations, who have the benefit of these experiences and relationships, can be right where they want to be after just one weekend and an ongoing commitment to a LinkedIn strategy. That's how I started six short years ago. I got on LinkedIn.com, bought a few books, digested the information, and was on my way to creating my own LinkedIn strategy.

Let me address the components of the Power Formula in greater detail so you can better grasp its importance.

Your Unique Experience

Every one of us has unique experiences that we bring to the marketplace. These experiences include our education, jobs, culture, ethnicity, interests, and family, to name a few. Today, with virtual marketing and promotion more important than ever, developing a strong personal brand is essential, and your unique experience is a substantial component of that brand. The longer you have been in the marketplace, the more experiences you have amassed, each of which may come to bear on your next business opportunity.

Your Unique Relationships

Because none of us has walked the same path or encountered the same people, we have each developed a unique set of relationships. These relationships have been the foundation of our friendships, business partnerships, and customer bases. When we need help, whether personally or professionally, we turn to these people—our network. They in turn know that we are just a phone call away when we have the knowledge, experience, or resources to assist them. Our networks are one of our most valuable possessions, and as they continue to expand and diversify, they become even more important to our business and personal lives.

The Tool

The tool could be anything that helps accelerate or "power up" your ability to accomplish your goals, and social media tools certainly fall into this category. Traditionally, when the old tool is "working just fine," we can be reluctant to embrace the new tool, despite its promise to be better, faster, or perhaps even cheaper. For instance, your old, paper address book (the tool) worked just fine, but you eventually made the switch to a new tool—perhaps Microsoft Outlook. The process of learning to use the new tool may have been challenging at first, but your commitment and persistence were rewarded when you finally figured out how to retrieve all that valuable information with the click of a button.

So, why did I take all this time to share with you my revelation about the Power Formula when I told you I would be teaching you about the capabilities and functions of LinkedIn? Because I want you to understand that the **unique experience** you have gained coupled with the **unique relationships** you have carefully developed gives you a tremendous advantage over the person who understands **the tool** (in this case, LinkedIn) but is only beginning to gain experience and develop professional relationships.

Am I trying to discourage those of you who are younger business professionals or just starting your business careers? No way! This book will help you understand how to begin to develop your personal brand by creating a compelling LinkedIn profile and expand your network in order to accomplish your professional goals.

To help you keep focused on the Power Formula as you read this book, there will be a box at the end of each chapter that reemphasizes key points in terms of your **unique experience** and **unique relationships**. These sections will help you define your own power formula for succeeding in whatever you hope to accomplish in your career.

CHAPTER 2

The Million-Cubicle Project
LinkedIn—Making the Invisible Visible

LinkedIn has described their mission as follows: "Connect the world's professionals to make them more productive and successful. When you join LinkedIn, you get access to people, jobs, news, updates, and insights that help you be great at what you do." Let me start by addressing how LinkedIn works from a practical standpoint.

In their current user agreement, LinkedIn states, "You agree that you will not invite people you do not know to join your network." In earlier versions of the user agreement, they referred to "your network of trusted professionals." They are obviously encouraging their members to only connect with people they know. This is where LinkedIn differs significantly from social media sites like Facebook, where members attempt to get as many "friends" as they can—and where the word *friend* is loosely defined. With LinkedIn, the goal is to connect with only those people whom you consider to be trusted professionals. That leads to the first strategic decision you have to make: You need to personally decide whom you will consider a trusted professional based on the strategy you intend to pursue on LinkedIn. Some people choose to focus on expanding their networks even if this means embracing a loose definition of the word *trusted*. In contrast, I like to say a person is trusted if I can pick up the phone and ask him for a favor or an introduction and be confident that he would say "yes," or if he is someone for whom I would do the same.

The person you just met in the vegetable aisle at your local grocery store typically does not meet my standard of a trusted professional. He might be a nice person and you may have enjoyed the two minutes of conversation, but that doesn't qualify him as "trusted" when he runs home and decides to look for you on LinkedIn. The decision about who is "trusted" is a very important starting point with LinkedIn, and there are lots of debates about this matter. However, in my opinion, most LinkedIn users will be best served by following a more conservative definition of trusted. I will provide additional comments and thoughts later on the always-raging debate between quality and quantity as it relates to your network.

Once you have opened a LinkedIn account and begun connecting with your trusted friends and colleagues, your database on LinkedIn begins to grow in ways that are obvious (your number of connections gets larger) but also in ways that are not so obvious. In order to truly comprehend the power of LinkedIn, it is important to understand the part you cannot see—your extended network.

LinkedIn is constantly evolving, and the information shown in Figure 2.1 is no longer available on the LinkedIn site in this form, but I include it here to help you visualize degrees of separation—the Kevin Bacon concept that we are all connected by six degrees of separation or less to virtually everyone in the world. You will notice here that there are three circled numbers: 1, 2, and 3. The first group is one degree away from you; these are your personal connections, labeled with the subheading "Your trusted friends and colleagues."

Figure 2.1: LinkedIn makes your extended network visible.

Your Network of Trusted Professionals

You are at the center of your network. Your connections can introduce you to 5,775,100+ professionals — here's how your network breaks down:

1 Your Connections Your trusted friends and colleagues		1,190
2 Two degrees away Friends of friends; each connected to one of your connections		109,800+
3 Three degrees away Reach these users through a friend and one of their friends		5,664,000+
Total users you can contact through an Introduction		5,775,100+

8,497 new people in your network since April 16

Here is an example of how first-degree connections work. Let's say I have a friend named Joe Smith. Joe and I have been friends for a long time. Maybe we hung out in the rain at our kids' soccer games or perhaps we are close business associates. I decide that Joe and I should connect on LinkedIn. I search for his name, find him, and extend an invitation to Joe, asking him to join my LinkedIn network. Once Joe accepts my invitation, he does not need to turn around and invite me into his network as well. At that point, we are both connected to each other at the first level.

Your first-degree connections should be people who are already part of your offline network. You have a network that you have built over the course of your lifetime, whether that be high school, college, places you worked, clubs to which you belong, or acquaintances you have made in your day-to-day life. This is what I call your "flat" network. The premise of LinkedIn is that you transform your "flat" list of contacts into a dynamic, multidimensional network. Putting your contacts into LinkedIn will enable you to access additional degrees of depth within your network and will allow your contacts to assist you in new and valuable ways.

Let's go back to Joe Smith, my first-degree connection. When I owned an office furniture dealership, if Joe were building a building and needed my products and services, he would probably call me because I know him so well. The fun begins when you think about the second degree. Let's say Joe Smith knows Bob Anderson. I have never met Bob Anderson. However, let's say that Bob is going to build a new building in town, and rumor has it that this building will contain over a million cubicles. As a furniture guy, a million-cubicle job in a town the size of mine would be a *really* big deal. Your equivalent of my million-cubicle sale might be finding the perfect job, meeting a strategic partner who will bring you additional revenue, finding a vendor that will enable you to decrease your production costs, or connecting with a foundation or individual who is interested in assisting your favorite charity.

Let's say I hear that Bob's company, The Anderson Company, is going to construct this building, and I put either "Bob Anderson" or "The Anderson Company" into the LinkedIn search engine and find out that my friend Joe Smith is connected to Bob Anderson. I find this out because when I do a search, I see that Bob's name is next to a "2nd" icon, which means he knows one of my Number 1 connections. I may know some of Joe's friends—having golfed, gone to parties, or hung out with many of them—but I definitely don't know all of them. For this example, let's assume I do not know Bob and do not know how he knows my friend Joe.

So, learning of this connection after searching LinkedIn, I excitedly call Joe and ask him if he would connect me with his friend Bob Anderson, to which he replies, "Are you kidding? Of course. He's a good friend of mine. We've been friends for a long, long time. If my connecting you with Bob can help you, I'd love to do it." Isn't that what networks have always done? The added benefit of LinkedIn is that I can now see a list of Joe's connections and request an introduction to any of his connections I would like to meet.

Stop and think about the power of that. Without LinkedIn, what are the chances I would know that Joe Smith knows Bob Anderson? But with this tool, I can find it out almost immediately and can then use my network to connect with Bob.

Let's take it one step further, to the third degree, and imagine that Bob Anderson is friends with Jill Jones. Remember that I don't know Bob or Jill—I only know Joe. However, I now have the ability to search Jill Jones and The Jones Company, only to find out that Jill is building a building with—you guessed it—a million cubicles. I now have a chance to talk with her by contacting Joe, who contacts Bob, who contacts Jill.

Let's just take a look at the total number of people I had access to through LinkedIn at the time I captured this screenshot (see Figure 2.2). Joe is a first-degree connection, Bob is a second-degree connection, and Jill is a third-degree connection, and I had 1,190 Joes, 109,800 Bobs, and over 5.6 million people in the Jill Jones category. These numbers never cease to amaze me. Sometimes I think there must be some dogs and cats in those numbers—there's no way I could be connected to that many businesspeople. However, at this point I actually did have over 5.7 million human connections (no cats or dogs!), many of whom may just lead me to that million-cubicle sale. I always had over 5.7 million people in my extended network; I just never knew who they were and how they were connected to me. And my network has grown exponentially since this point.

Figure 2.2: Your network grows exponentially.

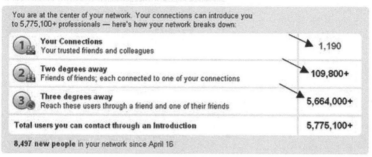

Remember the good old-fashioned method of networking? If I wanted to get ahold of either Bob Anderson or Jill Jones to talk about a potential business opportunity, I would be calling them (if I even knew their names) and sending e-mails, letters, postcards, whatever. The other thirteen furniture dealers who are located in my town would undoubtedly be using the same tactics. This would probably result in Bob and Jill screaming, "No more furniture guys!" With LinkedIn, I can have a friend or a friend of a friend assist me in making a contact that would typically be extremely difficult to coordinate. This is the number one power of LinkedIn: It takes connections that would normally be invisible and makes them visible.

Now let me give you an example of what could happen if you and your contacts choose to embrace the strategy of using a more casual definition of the word *trusted*. Say I am very excited about the opportunity of a cubicle sale because when I searched Bob Anderson and his company, I found that he is a second-degree connection. I call my first-degree connection, Joe Smith, and Joe says, "I don't think I know him. Who is Bob?"

"Bob Anderson," I say. "He is connected to you on LinkedIn. Of course you know him."

"Wayne, I really don't know him."

"You've got to be kidding me. He's a first-degree connection with you on LinkedIn. I can see it. How can you not know somebody in your network?"

If that happens several times, I might say to Joe, "Your network stinks. You really don't know anybody you're connected to. You just have a whole bunch of names in there, and you don't have any deep relationships with anyone. You're like a kid on Facebook."

That's why I stick with the premise that for most people, your network should be made up of people you know and trust; it allows you to help people. When you get to three degrees away, you hope the relationship that exists between yourself and your first-degree connection is as strong as the first to the second and the second to the third. If not, the connective power of LinkedIn can be greatly diminished.

The majority of books and blogs on the subject of networking say most business professionals have between 200 and 250 people they consider trusted professionals. If you're not on LinkedIn, these contacts are probably kept and managed in some kind of document or file, such as a Microsoft Outlook file on your computer, a card file, a list of names of people, a box of business cards in the top drawer of your desk, etc. All I am asking you to consider doing is taking those 200 to 250 contacts and getting them into LinkedIn. That way, you will not only have those 200 to 250 first-degree contacts; you will also gain the ability to know who their Number 1's and their Number 2's are. Your contacts' Number 1's and Number 2's then become your Number 2's and Number 3's. At this point, the number of people in your LinkedIn network can get incredibly large, as you saw in the previous example.

Let me stop and ask you this question: Can you have too many first-degree connections? If you answered yes, you are mostly correct. But let me ask the question differently: Can you have too many Number 1's as long as each one is trusted? The answer is no—as long as they are trusted, you cannot have too many first-degree connections, and you shouldn't second-guess the potential significance of what that Number 1 does, where he lives, or what his background is. That is not the point. As long as he fits your criterion of being trusted, make him a first-degree connection so that you can find out whom he is connected to—and potentially connect with all of his connections and his connections' connections. You have no idea who she plays golf with every Saturday or who he sat next to in church last Sunday.

In the past few years, I have read countless books, blogs, and commentaries about LinkedIn, and the quality versus quantity issue is continually debated by authors. This is the question of whether it's better to have a huge network of people you do not know very well or a smaller network of people with whom you are well acquainted. I consistently teach that your network should be made up primarily of trusted professionals. However, I do think there are certain circumstances in which you may decide to stretch that rule for strategic reasons.

One example is recruiters. Because they are in the "body business," they need sizeable inventories of people with varied backgrounds and strengths; therefore, it makes sense for them to have very large networks. I actually heard about one international recruiter who has 30,000 first-level connections. Sales professionals who are responsible for very large territories are another segment of users who many times choose quantity over quality. Personally, now that my book is available in three languages and my LinkedIn consulting business has taken on a more national scope, I have found it beneficial to strategically expand my network as well. You may be in a similar situation that makes you decide to stretch the "trusted professional" rule. My feeling is that as long as you have thoroughly considered your decision, more power to you for using LinkedIn strategically.

When I was a full-time Milwaukee furniture guy, I would occasionally invite people into my network even though I just met them the previous day at a networking event. This was typically the result of either having had an interesting conversation with the person or having reason to believe further contact with him or her could lead to a mutually beneficial business relationship. Included with these immediate invitations would be a list of times I was available to meet for coffee or lunch so that we could continue to develop our relationship. These are what I call work-in-progress Number 1 connections. I would work very hard at building these relationships to a point where I believed the person qualified as a trusted professional.

As mentioned before, the real power of LinkedIn is that it takes connections that are normally invisible and makes them visible. Make your connections visible by transforming your "flat," offline network into a dynamic, multidimensional network of trusted professionals, and you will be on your way to securing that million-cubicle project.

APPLYING THE POWER FORMULA

- Your first step is to define what constitutes a trusted profes-sional. I would suggest writing this definition down. These people make up that very important first part of the Power Formula: your **unique relationships.**

- Remember, with each new first-level connection you add, that person's Number 1's become new Number 2's in your network, and their Number 2's become new Number 3's in your network. That multiplication process helps you grow your **unique** network exponentially.

CHAPTER 3

Where's the Beef?

The LinkedIn Profile: Basics

Everyone starts on LinkedIn with a profile. A profile can be as simple as your name. However, if you choose to list little but your name, you will be missing a tremendous opportunity to avail yourself of the two major benefits of a LinkedIn profile: the ability to be found and the opportunity to tell your story.

Plain and simple, profiles should be beefy. For those readers who are old enough, think of the Wendy's commercial from the eighties in which the elderly ladies asked "Where's the beef?" as they looked at a tiny hamburger patty dwarfed by a massive bun. For those of you who are not familiar with the commercial, check it out on YouTube. You'll find it quite entertaining.

There are four reasons you want your profile to be beefy:

1. Your LinkedIn profile is a place where you can tell your story completely and fully, so that when people are

looking at your profile, they will be encouraged to do business with you over your competitors. They will see the depth and breadth of your experience, your professional recommendations, and the brands you carry, plus your certifications, educational experience, and all the other qualifications you possess that make you the obvious professional to do business with in the marketplace you serve. I like to refer to a LinkedIn profile as a "resume on steroids."

In contrast to a traditional resume, which is typically a listing of facts and dates, your LinkedIn profile allows you the opportunity to tell your story. It should be a narrative of sorts, where you emphasize your experience and high level of credibility. This "resume on steroids" should shout out "I'm the best at this in my market!"

To help tell your story, you can include details about yourself that, while perhaps bordering on personal information, will get across to the viewer who you are as a unique individual. For example, one of my class attendees told me that through the LinkedIn profile of a prospective client, he learned the guy collected wines—and he also found out which one was his favorite. On the day following his proposal presentation, he followed up with a thank-you note and included a bottle of—you guessed it—his prospective client's favorite wine, and the rest is history. He got the order.

2. Every word in your profile is keyword searchable. Thus, having a beefy profile will increase your chances of being found. As you know from using Google, keyword

searching on the Internet is an extremely powerful tool for finding people. Similarly, searching on LinkedIn can produce extremely valuable results. The search function enables you to find people who have certain types of experience, classifications, and/or brands. In subsequent chapters, I will address in detail how you can increase the likelihood of being found on LinkedIn by strategically including specific information and keywords in the various sections of your profile.

When I owned the office furniture dealership, I was looking for a person interested in bicycling to join a group of cyclists for a charity event my company was sponsoring. Discovering a bicycling enthusiast who happens to be an architect or builder would be a home run. I would then be able to advance a professional relationship, help a charitable organization, *and* enjoy a day of bicycling. Therefore, I searched the words *builder, architect, cycling,* and *bicycling* and instantly had my choice of architects and builders with whom to spend the day. Without those keywords in their profiles, none of these people would have been found. The power of searching is discussed in detail in Chapter 10.

3. A beefy profile shows that you are not a dinosaur. What do I mean by this? For those of us in the Baby Boomer generation, people tend to appreciate the experience we possess, but they are also interested in knowing whether we are keeping abreast of the latest trends in the business world, including social media. A beefy profile will demonstrate you are on top of current trends in your profession

or occupation and you embrace technology. You are *not* a dinosaur.

4. You should expect your profile to regularly be compared with those of your competitors. Therefore, in order to gain a competitive advantage, you will want your profile to include a plethora of information, keywords, and details about who you are, what you hope to accomplish, and how you might be able to assist others.

    Many savvy LinkedIn users will review a person's profile before meeting with her for the first time. Personally, I always talk about common interests, mutual friends, or some other interesting fact I found on her profile before I jump into, "So, I hear you need some LinkedIn training." Business professionals use their LinkedIn profiles to tell their stories. As a result, it can be extremely beneficial to review the profile of the potential customer, prospective employee, vendor, or other person with whom you desire to have a business relationship. Because of the vast amount of information available on the Internet in general and on LinkedIn in particular, it has become commonplace to "shop" several vendors online before engaging in direct communication.

    Do yourself a favor and take a look at the profiles of some of your competitors. Observe what they are saying about themselves—awards they have won, certifications they hold, types of projects they have worked on, etc.—because this may jog your memory and remind you of similar information you could include in your profile. Based on the information contained in the profiles, would a potential customer be encouraged to do business with you as opposed to one of your competitors? If you think your competitor would get the nod, then start beefing up your profile.

Now that you know the reasons you want your profile to be beefy, the next several chapters will show you the steps to making sure you have all the necessary information on your profile.

APPLYING THE POWER FORMULA

- It will be awfully hard for you to delegate the step of creating a beefy profile to someone else. No one knows your story like you do or can feel as passionate about why that story makes you the best at what you do. That passion will be evident if you personally craft a beefy profile that explains your **unique experience.**

- Try not to turn your profile into a bunch of marketing gobbledygook. People want to read about what you have done in a simple, understandable format. You need to impress them with what you have accomplished, not with how many buzzwords you can include.

- Start to assemble the details of your **unique experience** by reviewing all of your past jobs and awards, but do not wait to get going on this until you think you have it all together. Subsequent additions to your profile are not only fine but preferable. I will address that topic in more detail later in this book.

Take full advantage of every space on your profile with the help of the handy tip sheet "It's All About Character: Take Full Advantage of Every Space," available on page 185.

CHAPTER 4

Your 10-Second Bumper Sticker

The LinkedIn Profile:
Personal Identification Box

The first item on your LinkedIn profile is what I like to refer to as your "top box" (see Figure 4.1). This box identifies you with several key pieces of information, including your name, headline, photograph, location, industry, experience, education, websites, and contact information. In this chapter I will address the three most prominent items—name, photo, and headline—because this information is used to identify you throughout the LinkedIn site. Some people will never go to your profile to look at the details, but they will see your personal identification box—what I like to refer to as your "10-second bumper sticker" (see Figure 4.2). Let's address those components one at a time.

Figure 4.1: Your top box is front and center on your profile. Follow my guidelines and make a great first impression.

Figure 4.2: A businesslike photo and compelling headline will help you achieve maximum impact from your 10-second bumper sticker.

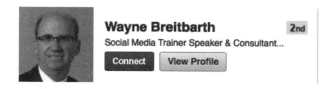

Your Name

This element is pretty self-explanatory. Your name should include nothing but your full name, unless you have high-level academic degrees or easily recognizable certifications, such as PhD, MD, CPA, and certain other high-level insurance classifications or nursing classifications, etc. Personally, I wouldn't include designations on the level of an MBA.

Since there will undoubtedly be people who will only know them by their maiden names, some married women who have taken on their husband's last name find it useful to list a maiden name in parentheses—for example, Susan (Jones) Cunningham.

You can also list your maiden name, former name, or nickname on your profile by using the Former Name field. To access this, go to "Profile" on the top toolbar. Click the pencil icon next to your name, choose "Former Name," and fill in the box. Then choose whether you want this name visible to only your first-level connections, your entire network, or everyone on LinkedIn. Your former name will only appear in LinkedIn searches—not searches done on Internet search engines.

Your Photograph

Most LinkedIn experts are in agreement on the importance of including a photograph in your profile, as well as the benefit of using a headshot (professionally taken or near professional quality) of yourself wearing business attire, smiling, and looking like a person with whom people would want to do business. In fact, LinkedIn suggests you are fourteen times more likely to have your profile viewed if you have a photo.

Let's talk about why personal photographs are a hang-up for some people, especially members of the Baby Boomer generation. Plain and simple, we Baby Boomers are afraid to admit that we are in our fifties or sixties. Well, the reality is that you cannot hide behind the computer screen and pretend you are twenty-nine years old forever, and you surely are not going to be able to hide your age when you show up for the job interview or when you show up to collect the check for the order the customer placed after you found him on LinkedIn and put together the sale. So get over it!

Many times people will remember a face before they remember a name. I want to be the person people find on LinkedIn the day after they meet me at an event and say, "I really liked that bald LinkedIn guy. That's the guy. I recognize him by his picture." The person who recognizes you from your photo may be the one who leads you to your million-cubicle sale.

Your Headline

A basic headline consists of the company you work for and the position you hold there, but the headline field can contain 120 characters, and it is your opportunity to tell an abbreviated version of your story. In it, you will want to describe your experience and mention how you can help someone who sees your profile or 10-second bumper sticker. You can edit your headline by clicking the pencil icon next to your current headline.

For the first seven or eight months I was on LinkedIn, my headline read, "President and Owner, M&M Office Interiors, where we give you the space you want and the experience you deserve, and LinkedIn trainer." "The space you want and the experience you deserve" is the tagline for the company I owned at the time. I loved my tagline. I paid a lot of money for my tagline. It was the result of very extensive research, and I definitely think it stands for the brand the company has in the marketplace. However, as much as I loved my tagline and what it says, it did not clearly state that my number-one priority was selling office furniture. So I changed my headline to "President, M&M Office Interiors, where we have served the office furniture market for over 50 yrs, and LinkedIn Trainer." It didn't incorporate my business's tagline, but it better described me as a business professional. Unless you work for a multinational corporation that is a household name, you cannot assume the readers of your profile will know what type of products or services you provide. It is imperative for your headline to clearly express what your company does and/or what your business proposition is.

If you have multiple jobs or a primary job and a secondary job, be sure to list all positions you hold. If you are looking for a job, your headline should clearly state that you are a job seeker looking for a position as an IT professional in the food manufacturing/distribution business, for example. If you do not enter a customized headline, LinkedIn will use your most recent job title and company name as your descriptive headline. But do take time to create a powerful headline; it could be the deciding factor in someone's choice to connect with you or look at the details in your full profile.

I personally prefer a narrative-type headline, but a popular alternative is a style that consists of keywords separated by the pipe symbol. To get the pipe symbol, use the shift key together with the backslash key. Some people choose this option because LinkedIn's current search ranking formula gives extra weight to the words in your headline. Because you only have 120 characters available for your headline, using the pipe symbol will allow you to put more keywords in your headline. I currently have three positions I want to include in my headline, and thus I've found it necessary to switch to the pipe key option, and my headline looks like this:

Social Media Trainer Speaker & Consultant | Author, THE POWER FORMULA FOR LINKEDIN SUCCESS | LinkedIn Expert

Whichever option you choose, include your most important keywords, so that when people search for the keywords you included, they will find you—and not your competitor who didn't think to put keywords in his headline.

In summary, I cannot overemphasize the importance of your 10-second bumper sticker. It will travel with you and be your identifier throughout LinkedIn. Be sure it is thorough and correct. If you do not have a photograph or a complete headline, you may cause someone to question your credibility or fail to thoroughly understand your business. As a result, he or she may choose to do business with someone else. Follow the steps I have outlined, and you will be on your way not only to a great 10-second bumper sticker but also to a terrific LinkedIn profile.

APPLYING THE POWER FORMULA

- Your goal with the headline is to create a compelling marketing statement about your **unique experience** in just 120 characters, while also including some critical keywords. Create a few drafts of your statement, and then ask several of your closest connections for a critique of what you have written.

- Do not use an outdated photo of yourself. You are attempting to demonstrate your **unique experience**, and experience comes with age. People need to see you in that photo and put that picture together with the person they just met or are going to meet.

Create a magnetic profile with the help of "Profile Perfection: A Checklist for LinkedIn Optimization," available on page 189.

You only get one chance to make a first impression. To learn how to impress viewers with your LinkedIn headline, download "The Definitive Worksheet to Optimize Your LinkedIn Profile Headline," available at **www.powerformula.net/free**.

CHAPTER 5

Resume on Steroids

The LinkedIn Profile: Experience Section

As mentioned earlier, I like to think of the LinkedIn profile as a "resume on steroids," and the section of your profile that most resembles a traditional resume is the Experience section. You will find this section in the middle of your profile, and some of the information in your Experience section is also summarized within the top box.

People often ask me what jobs they should put on their profiles. These are the criteria I suggest you use, not only for jobs but for anything else on your profile:

1. Does putting this on my profile add to my story or increase my credibility?
2. Does putting this on my profile make it easier for people to find me?

3. If I do not put this on my profile and my competitors have it on their profiles, will I be at a competitive disadvantage? In other words, will I be mad I didn't include it on mine?

4. Does this information help people understand what I do and how I can help them?

If the answer to any of these four questions is yes, then, by all means, include the position on your profile.

My recommendation is to put every job you have ever held on your profile. Begin each job entry with a descriptive title. Take full advantage of the 100 characters LinkedIn allows for the title of each entry in the Experience section. For example, one of my job titles is *CEO | Social Media Trainer and Strategy Consultant (specializing in LinkedIn)*. I could have simply said *CEO*, but this is a much better description of what I do—and the extra keywords (*social media, strategy, consultant, LinkedIn*) will help people find me.

It's important to use plenty of relevant keywords throughout your Experience section. You will also want to highlight not only your present area of expertise but also any specialties relating to previous positions. This is important because when someone searches LinkedIn for a professional with experience in multiple disciplines, the combination of keywords will increase your chances of being found.

It is very important to spend plenty of time crafting the job descriptions on your profile. All too often people fail to spend sufficient time on this because the detail of previous jobs in the Experience section shows up so far down the page, and they are tired or anxious to move on to other tasks. Do not make this mistake. You never know which job experience or accomplishment will put you ahead of the other candidates in the eyes of a potential customer or employer. And if certain keywords show up multiple times on your profile because you use them in multiple job descriptions, you will be listed higher in the search results, which is definitely a good thing.

Once you've crafted descriptive titles for the positions you've held, describe your jobs in detail—the position you held, what you accomplished, and what experience you gained—and include a list of awards you received while you held each job. You can impress readers further with a timeline of the promotions you received at each job. And if you *really* want to wow them, describe the type of customers or clients you serve(d) and include a killer quote from one of your satisfied customers. The goal here is to add interest and credibility to your story—not simply list your job duties.

When you describe your accomplishments, it's also important to emphasize your diverse experience and ability to complete important tasks. Include any statistics or impressive results you've achieved. Also, highlight experience that aligns with your current and future goals. This will show readers that you are qualified to help them now and in the future.

You will also notice that on my profile I have listed several volunteer positions (see Figure 5.1). Viewers of my profile can see I am actively involved in giving back to my community, and most of us like to hire and work with people who care about others. This is another way to impress viewers of your profile prior to a face-to-face meeting or telephone call. For job seekers, listing volunteer positions and relevant extracurricular experience is a must. For new graduates, where actual job experience may be in short supply, this is your way of showing potential employers that you have been actively involved with specific organizations, worked as part of a team, held leadership positions, and contributed to your community. I prefer to list some of my charitable activities in the Experience section because then they will appear closer to the top

Figure 5.1: Improve your credibility by including your volunteer positions.

Board Member
The Community Warehouse
January 2007 – Present (6 years)

Community Warehouse is a non-profit, faith-based provider set up to serve people in the Milwaukee community with affordable home and facility improvement materials. Our goal is to partner with foundations, non-profits, individuals, builders, contractors, manufacturers and retailers to provide the resources that are needed for rebuilding Milwaukee's under-resourced communities and as a result, significantly improve the quality of life in our neighborhoods.

Whether it's a simple home improvement project or drastic renovation, Community Warehouse is committed to helping our members in any way possible. We believe that self-respect and dignity come from having a safe and pleasant home to grow in. We're doing our job when our members are proud of their place and happy to be home.

Community Warehouse's focus is to provide relief to Milwaukee neighborhoods in need. We want to turn areas into neighborhoods and houses into homes. Together, we're offering hope and changing lives one household at a time.

Founder, Volunteer High School Mentor
Urban Promise Lunch Club
October 2008 – Present (4 years 3 months)

We meet at Ronald Reagan High School, an MPS school on the south side of Milwaukee. We have lunch, a short talk/speaker, and then meet with students one on one to help them with life issues, college selection/criteria, jobs, and anything else the students want to talk about. We are always looking for additional mentors/volunteers. Contact me if you are interested in being part of our team.

of my profile. In Chapter 9 I discuss using an add-on profile section called Volunteer Experience & Causes—another great place to list (and promote) your favorite organizations.

Another reason for listing all jobs you have held is that recommendations must be attached to a job or education entry; a person cannot post a general recommendation to your profile. Therefore, every job listing gives you another opportunity to include an enthusiastic recommendation from a trusted colleague, professor, previous employer, or satisfied customer.

The Experience section is an extremely important component of your "resume on steroids." It gives you an opportunity to tell the story of who you are as a professional. Spend a significant amount of time writing a detailed description for all jobs listed—and don't forget the keywords. Then step back, review your entries, and ask yourself, *Would I hire me as an employee or vendor?* If the answer is "no," then go back and beef up your job entries!

APPLYING THE POWER FORMULA

- In order to be sure each entry you make on your profile thoroughly explains your **unique experience**, try to think of each job as if it were the only one you ever had. This will help you get very detailed in terms of experience, accomplishments, awards, responsibilities, etc. Sometimes we tend to cut corners because, in total, the profile looks fine. However, you never know which of those details presented in a job listing will resonate with the reader of your profile or be the important keywords that help someone find you.

CHAPTER 6

Put Your Best Foot Forward

The LinkedIn Profile: Additional Top Box Items

In this chapter I will cover the remaining items included in the top box of your LinkedIn profile. These entries are front and center in an abbreviated form when someone views your profile, and the detail is listed further down on your profile.

Your Location and Industry

This component of your top box represents the location and industry in which you do business. LinkedIn will assign you a region based on the zip code you provide, but you will need to manually select your industry from the list LinkedIn provides. The industries currently offered by LinkedIn are not very specific in some cases, but they are adding more all the time. For example, "office furniture" is not on the list at this time. Because M&M Office Interiors provides interior design services, its employees could select "design." However, they choose "furniture" because it more accurately describes their industry. If LinkedIn does not currently have a category for your industry, I suggest you check on a regular basis to see if they've added an industry designation that more closely fits your business.

Education

I recommend that you list all the education you have had, including high school, college, and any significant additional education you received that relates to your industry and/or specialty. One of the benefits of listing all your educational background is that when you are looking to add lots of connections in a hurry—which we will discuss in a subsequent chapter—LinkedIn helps you use the schools or other institutions you attended as a way of finding people with whom you might like to connect.

People sometimes ask me why I would want to list my high school. The first reason is that it can help people find you. The second reason is that people tend to like to do business with fellow alumni, whether they are from high school or college. You cannot predict why a person might select you over your competitors, but a common educational experience could be the deciding factor. So, do yourself a favor and list all schools you have attended.

Under each educational entry, include specific information regarding what your degrees required and what credibility you have because of those degrees. This could include specific classes, internships, leadership roles, study abroad experiences, or anything else you feel shows that your educational experience was more comprehensive than simply completing the coursework required to receive a degree or certification. This is another great way to add credibility to each and every entry on your profile.

You can also list significant industry-specific classes, workshops, or seminars you have attended by clicking "Add education," which you'll find right below your other education entries. In the "School" box, type the name of the school or organization that provided the training or education. When you begin typing the name, LinkedIn will show you a list of all schools that are already in their database. When you choose your school from the list, the school's logo will show up on your profile. You can then type in whatever information about that opportunity you feel will enhance your credibility (see Figure 6.1). An added benefit to listing every educational experience is, of course, the opportunity to receive recommendations for each of these entries.

Figure 6.1: Enhance your credibility by highlighting nontraditional educational experiences.

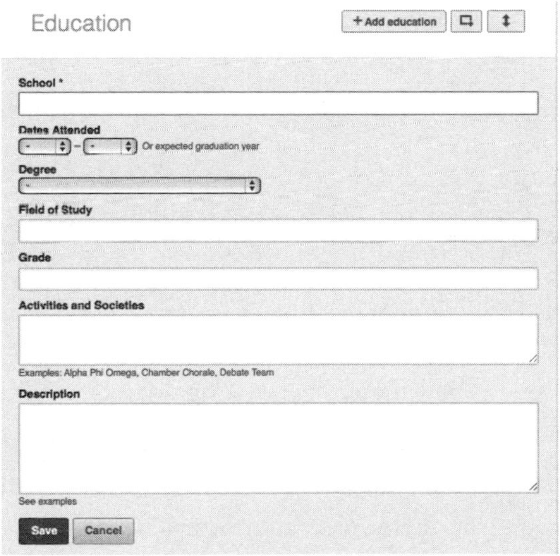

Contact Information

This section is very important but somewhat hidden. If you click the Contact Info box (see Figure 6.2), you can add your contact information, including e-mail, phone, IM, address, websites, and Twitter. Include whichever ones you use consistently and feel comfortable sharing. Your first-level connections will see all of this information. However, other people will only be able to see your websites and Twitter information.

Figure 6.2: How much contact information you share is up to you.

Websites

Included in the Contact section is Websites, which contains hyperlinks to specific web pages. People typically have only one thing listed here, most often the website of the company they work for, and the link is usually titled "My Company." Your company's website is a good place to start, but there is a lot of marketing opportunity going to waste if you stop there. You can designate up to three links. Linking enables you to direct people to wherever you would like them to go, giving you the opportunity to send people not only to your company website but also to, for example, a sign-up sheet where they can get on your mailing list. You can link to videos, on YouTube or elsewhere on the web, and you can link to other social media sites like Facebook, your blog, etc.

Websites is also a great place to display additional areas of interest, such as organizations and charities in which you are involved, and you will be promoting these organizations' websites by adding them to your profile. You have lots of flexibility here, and you *do not* have to list the URL of your LinkedIn profile as one of the three sites. Using all three for links to other websites will also move your LinkedIn profile up in the search results of sites like Google, Bing, and the other search engines.

Be sure to describe each of these websites. Most people don't realize they have this option and go with the default of "Personal Website," "Company Website," or "Blog." In reality, you can describe your websites with up to thirty characters. Don't miss this opportunity to brand these websites and give one more little marketing push about what you do and what you stand for. You can alter the website's description by selecting "Other:" in the pull-down menu and then typing the new description in the box next to the link (see Figure 6.3).

Figure 6.3: Creative website descriptions will encourage readers to take a look at your websites.

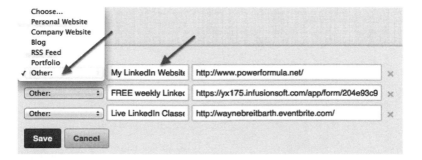

Public Profile URL

When you join LinkedIn, you in effect create your own one-page website—your LinkedIn profile. If you look at Figure 6.4, you will see an example of a URL that LinkedIn automatically assigned to a profile. Notice that it includes the user's name and several other seemingly random characters. LinkedIn does, however, allow you to assign your profile a more descriptive URL, and most people choose to simply add their name after www.LinkedIn.com/in/ (see Figure 6.5). To change your URL, click the settings icon next to your public profile URL. Then click the pencil on the top right next to "Your public profile URL," and type in your name. I'm lucky to have a unique name that no one had claimed yet, but you may find that your name has been taken. If that's the case, you can add a middle initial or a number following your name in order to save the URL. Changing this address to something closer to your actual name provides a more professional appearance when you use the URL on your resume, letterhead, and/or business card so that people can easily access your profile—your "resume on steroids."

Figure 6.4: Your initial public profile URL includes random numbers and characters.

Figure 6.5: A personalized LinkedIn URL will enhance your marketing and branding efforts.

This brings up a point you should understand: When you build a personal LinkedIn profile, you automatically create a public profile, which can be seen by anyone on the Internet who visits your URL. However, you can control exactly how much information is in the public domain, which I refer to as the "Google world," and how much you share only with the LinkedIn community. If you have a photograph on your LinkedIn profile, you can choose to omit the picture from your public profile so that people searching on Google cannot see it. When people are searching on Google or other search engines, your public LinkedIn profile will typically come up on the first page—hopefully it is the very first thing that shows up—but it does not need to have all the same content as your LinkedIn profile. Immediately beneath the place where you created your public profile URL, you can choose what information you'd like to display to the general public by checking or unchecking the boxes (see Figure 6.6).

Figure 6.6: Take control of how much information you share with the general public.

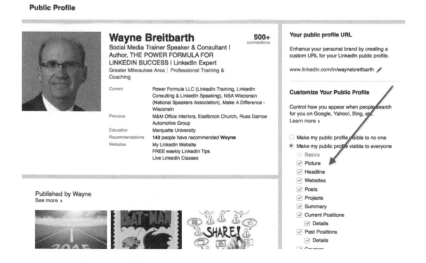

I choose to put everything that I have on my LinkedIn profile on my public profile. I keep my profile very professional, and I want all that information to be in the Google world. That way, if a person is not on LinkedIn, he can still see all the pertinent information about me, all the experiences I have had, the total number of recommendations I have received, and so on. You'll have to decide how much of this information you want to have available in the Google world, and if you stick with a very businesslike LinkedIn profile, you should be able to put almost everything on your public profile as well.

The items that complete your top box—your location and industry, education, contact info, websites, and public profile URL—are crucial to enhancing your credibility and improving the functionality of your LinkedIn profile. Don't lose energy and neglect to fill them in just because you're getting close to the bottom of your profile. They are all things that could make you stand out as better than the other guy. Be sure to spend the time and effort to craft them carefully and thoughtfully.

APPLYING THE POWER FORMULA

- Do not downplay or forget to include the details of your educational entries; they are an important descriptor of your **unique experience.** With 2,000 characters per job or educational entry, you have a lot of space to use. Remember, integrating keywords into your profile is part of the goal here as well.

- Your current company's website should be your first entry in the Websites section. This will add to the description of your **unique experience**—especially if the website includes customer profiles, a company history, descriptions of what your company does, etc.

- I cannot emphasize enough the importance of including industry-specific workshops, certifications, and training courses as key components of your **unique experience**. It just takes a few moments, and there's a really good chance that your competitors have missed this opportunity, despite the fact that they may have the same experience. This can be a great differentiator.

Share websites that will generate interest, increase credibility, and provide business leads with the help of the checklist "LinkedIn's Websites Section: Your 'Link' to Future Opportunities," available on page 193.

CHAPTER 7

That's My Boy!

The LinkedIn Profile: Summary Section

This chapter will concentrate on the most important section of your LinkedIn profile outside of the top box: the section right below the top box labeled "Summary." If you opened your LinkedIn account before 2012, you may also have a "Specialties" subheading within this section of your profile (more on this later). I have analyzed hundreds of profiles, and I continue to be amazed by how underutilized these two sections are; they can be so powerful in explaining your personal and business brand to viewers of your profile. The keywords included in them can also be very beneficial in helping people find you.

Summary Section

I like to think of this section as your cover letter, because in it you address the reader just as you would in a traditional cover letter. You can also use the summary to direct people to other sections of your profile and emphasize or summarize information you have detailed elsewhere.

The Summary section can contain up to 2,000 characters, and I recommend taking full advantage of every available character. If you write this section in narrative format, I suggest you use first person, as if you were talking directly to the person reading your profile. Another option is to compose the section in a concise, bulleted format. I prefer the narrative format because it allows you to write as you would speak, giving the section a conversational feel.

If you do write the Summary section in narrative format, consider the specific items you need to cover and the major topics you want to address. You may have several businesses and/or interests you want to highlight in this section of your profile, but this isn't a place to list every detail of every job you've ever had. Save that information for each respective job description in the Experience section, where you get 2,000 characters for every job. You can summarize some of your work experience in this section, but it is best to use your first paragraph to outline what you are trying to accomplish as a professional, who your perfect customer is, or other information that will help the reader relate to you. After reading the first paragraph of your summary, you want the reader to say, "I'd love to meet this person."

If you are a job seeker, this section should start off with a few sentences outlining the types of jobs that would be a perfect fit for your knowledge and skills. The remainder of the summary should describe why your experience has led you to that conclusion. Include details about how you have saved your previous employers money or increased productivity. You should explain these achievements in the Experience section, but you should also briefly highlight them here as well; some people may not make it down to the detailed job description, and this will be your only chance to tell them about that achievement. If you are a job seeker who is changing career paths, this is the place to explain why you have decided to make a change after years in a different industry or company.

These are some of the topics you may want to include in this section, depending on what your strategy is:

- What makes you, your company, and your products unique
- A description of your perfect customer, vendor relationship, employee, etc.
- A brief summary of the types of job experiences you have had
- Highlights of specific (hopefully quantifiable) things you have accomplished
- An excerpt from a letter of recommendation or testimonial, especially if you have not been able to obtain a LinkedIn recommendation from the person who wrote it
- Some of your hobbies or interests and why they make you a desirable employee or business partner
- Steps the reader can take to get further information on some of your accomplishments, projects you have completed, or awards you have won
- Why you think your experiences make you qualified for this next career step if you're a job seeker
- A brief description of any business relationships that have brought about superior results
- New markets you are considering going into and how viewers of your profile might fit into your plan
- A specific call to action so the reader knows what to do next (see the "Check out my website" section of my profile on page 56)

My LinkedIn Summary Section

Here is my LinkedIn summary, which will hopefully demonstrate the concepts discussed:

> I am a social media consultant, speaker, and trainer specializing in LinkedIn use and strategy. I have trained over 80,000 businesspeople—from entry level to CEO—on how to effectively use LinkedIn. I help companies develop a comprehensive strategy for using LinkedIn to grow their business and build their brand. I then train their team on how to use LinkedIn to meet their objectives.
>
> I am consistently asked to speak at Executive Agenda (EA), YPO, and TEC meetings, as well as CEO Roundtables and Renaissance Forums (REF), where my thirty years of experience as a business owner and manager enables me to help my peers understand how social media can benefit their companies. My diverse business experience also allows me to share real-life stores and illustrations as I educate, motivate, and entertain audiences at national conventions, industry events, and conferences.
>
> Check out my website at www.powerformula.net, where you can:
> - sign up to receive my FREE weekly social media tips
> - download lots of FREE social media resources
> - view some of my video presentations
> - read my blog
> - learn about the many services I provide for individuals and companies

** I AM NOT ENDORSED BY, CERTIFIED BY, SPONSORED BY, NOR AFFILIATED WITH LINKEDIN CORPORATION IN ANY WAY.

Your Summary section should be written so that if your mother read it, she would say, "That's my boy!" Make sure this "cover letter" section of your profile will be clearly understood by most people and it is not loaded with gobbledygook or jargon. Yes, you still need to be very conscious of the keywords that will put you in the search results you want to be in, but also be sure your story is well-told and the reader can clearly see the experiences and accomplishments that got you where you are in your career.

Since LinkedIn does not have a built-in spell-check, write this section in Microsoft Word or another word processor, do a spell-check, count the number of characters (remember, LinkedIn only allows 2,000), and then paste the contents of that document into LinkedIn, confident that your mother will be proud.

Specialties

Below the Summary section, you might have a subsection labeled "Specialties." I wish I could be more specific, but, as with most Internet sites, change is ongoing. At the time of this writing, I still have a Specialties section, but people with newer accounts do not have access to this section. LinkedIn does not always make changes and/or add new features across the board; rather, some users will see potential changes or additions in beta. But this is the first time I've seen current users retain a feature while newer users are not given access to the feature. Therefore, if you have a

Specialties section, don't delete it—you may not be able to get it back! And I'm hoping my Specialties section doesn't simply disappear some day, because I am maximizing my use of the 500 available characters in that section.

If you are a newer user and don't have a Specialties section, you should consider using part of your Summary section to list your specialties. You may also find it advantageous to put in a list of keywords as well. You will see an example of this in my Specialties section below.

I like to think of the Specialties section as a listing of your most important keywords. In my Specialties section, I begin with a comprehensive list of the keywords I want to be searched by. This is another way to ensure your name will come up as people search for topics relevant to what you do. Do not hesitate to repeat some of the keywords you included in the Summary section; using those keywords multiple times will move you up in the search rankings. As you list these keywords, be consistent with the identifiers you use in other materials—like company brochures, websites, and business cards—so there is consistency between all those marketing vehicles and your LinkedIn profile.

My LinkedIn Specialties Section

Here is what I've listed in my Specialties section. Notice that I included a frequent misspelling of my last name, which ensures I'll be found even if someone makes this common mistake. If the Specialties section is not available to you, I suggest you include common misspellings of your name in your Summary section.

KEYWORDS: Wisconsin, Milwaukee, LinkedIn, Christian, accountant, CPA, social media, trainer, teacher, instructor,

speaker, author, consultant, business development, networking, Brietbarth (sp), LinkedIn Power Formula

Corporate Consulting on LinkedIn
Corporate Training on LinkedIn
Speaking: conventions, industry events, keynote speaker

If you are a company owner, make sure all your employees who are
on LinkedIn use the same type of wording when describing the
company and its history and accomplishments. It is very important for a company to present a consistent, keyword-searchable
message throughout the LinkedIn universe.

You may find it beneficial to review the Summary and Specialties sections put forth by some of your competitors. Seeing
how they state their business proposition may assist you in thinking about how your business is different from theirs. Remember,
none of us has cornered the market on being the only smart guy
on LinkedIn. Learn from the profiles of your competitors—that
is one of the beauties of LinkedIn.

As I close this chapter, I want to emphasize an important point
that applies to your entire profile but tends to crop up most often
as people write their own Summary and Specialties sections: You
must be willing to brag about yourself when documenting your
accomplishments and experiences on your profile. If you have
trouble doing this, have someone else help you describe why you
are the perfect person for the job or why you should be the vendor
of choice. Remember this, too—your competitors will undoubtedly have no trouble bustin' their buttons with pride, so you'd better not be shy about bustin' yours.

APPLYING THE POWER FORMULA

- "Talk to me." That is the phrase I want you to keep top of mind as you write your Summary section. This is one of the few parts of your profile where you have a blank space and no specific boxes to fill in as you share the story of your **unique experience**.

- Take your current marketing materials (brochures, websites, handouts, etc.) and identify all the brands you represent, and include as many as possible in your Summary section.

- If your proposition is **unique**—for example, if you are the only person in your region representing a particular brand—make sure the person viewing your profile knows this by including this information in your Summary section.

- If you have **unique**, important terms that are often misspelled, consider including the misspelled form. That way, when someone searches by that misspelled word, you will still be found.

CHAPTER 8

Aren't You Any Good?

The LinkedIn Profile: Recommendations

Recommendations are a critical element of your profile for the following reasons:

1. Recommendations are outside verification of the information you have provided on your profile.
2. Words included in the recommendations are keyword searchable.
3. The number of recommendations you have is one of the weighting criteria in ranking search results on LinkedIn.

For these reasons, it is imperative that you get recommendations. I urge you—please, please, please, do not skip this important element of your profile. Spend time on it. Particularly if you are a job seeker, *do not* skip this part. It is one of the major things you will have going for you when it comes to the credibility of your profile.

If you are hesitant to go about getting recommendations, let me ask you this question: Aren't you any good? Of course you are. You, like most experienced businesspeople, have undoubtedly established a great reputation in your marketplace relating to the goods and/or services you provide. By working hard to get LinkedIn recommendations, you are simply documenting your great reputation so that people who review your profile will understand who you are and what you stand for, which is sure to result in improved business opportunities in the future.

Before he or she can post a LinkedIn recommendation on your profile, the person writing it must have a LinkedIn account and be connected to you. Therefore, if you have an important connection who is not on LinkedIn but who may be willing to write a LinkedIn recommendation for you, you might have to take some time to show him why he should be on LinkedIn, help him set up his profile, and then ask for the recommendation. You will be doing him a tremendous favor, and at the same time he will be helping you.

How Many Recommendations Should I Have?

I recommend that you seek out at least two recommendations for every job you have ever had. You should also seek out at least two recommendations for any work you have done with nonprofit organizations and for each educational experience, especially if you are a young business professional or in job-seeking mode. I suggest having at least two because two can be displayed with each job experience entry on your profile (See Figure 8.1). Many people assume that the more recommendations you have, the better you are at what you do. So get busy and secure those recommendations, bearing in mind that quality is as important as quantity.

Figure 8.1: Enhance your credibility by including impressive recommendations on your profile.

Check out a partial list of my talks at www.powerformula.net. I can also customize a talk just for you and your company or organization.

Contact me at wayne@powerformula.net for details.

▾ 8 recommendations, including:

 Sue Bennett
Marketing Specialist at First Bank

Wayne has inspired our office to be successful through LinkedIn and we are seeing the results! View↓

 Adam Loomis
President & CEO of National Bank

Wayne recently presented at one of bank's seminars and his presentation and message were absolutely top notch. He... View↓

6 more recommendations↓

What Should My Recommendations Say?

Recommendations should be specific and strategic, and you should attempt to get them from the most influential people willing to comment on each position you have held. Assist the person writing the recommendation by reminding her of some of the accomplishments, skills, or specific things you brought to the workplace. Many people are willing to write a recommendation but need to be reminded of your noteworthy accomplishments. Sending them a list of specific achievements and helpful keywords will not only make the task of writing a recommendation less time-consuming but may also result in a more accurate and effective recommendation.

Here is an example of a well-written recommendation I received from a person who purchased my online training course *Explode Your Revenues Using LinkedIn*:

> Wayne's new 6-module program teaches you everything you will ever need to know about LinkedIn and why you need to do certain actions on LinkedIn. Wayne's online course is very easy to use and is structured in small, two- or three-minute videos with screen shots and Wayne's enthusiastic teaching

commentary, which is like having Wayne sitting next to you, on demand, anytime.

Pick what LinkedIn topic you want to learn about, watch a brief video by Wayne, and immediately implement what you learn on each video. It's that simple. You can go at your own pace. The course includes many extra downloads, worksheets and PDFs which are very helpful.

Take advantage of all the power of LinkedIn and outperform your competition with Wayne Breitbarth by your side.

Why Are Recommendations So Important?

Recommendations are the only item on your profile that you do not personally write. And like most information on the Internet, profiles are only as trustworthy as the people who create them. Your friends and business associates obviously know you are a truthful person, but your profile will be viewed by many people who are unfamiliar with you. Therefore, recommendations are extremely important because they are outside verification of the information you have provided on your LinkedIn profile. I have had several people tell me that recommendations on their profile were a very significant factor in their ability to land the perfect job. In many cases, the hiring executive told them so.

Recommendations are also important because if a person writes a recommendation for you, your name and the fact that she recommended you will appear on her profile. It's really cool to think about your name popping up on someone else's profile, especially if she is a person of influence.

Tips for Getting Recommendations

So now you're probably thinking, *Where am I going to get all those recommendations? People don't do those anymore. I don't even know where my ex-boss is!* Do not overlook the fact that you can get recommendations from people besides your direct superior, such as a person who worked above your superior or the owner of the company. You could also ask a supplier or vendor for a recommendation. A customer with whom you have had an exceptionally strong relationship may be willing to write one for you. Last but not least are coworkers who can verify the specific points you want to emphasize about your background, experience, and work ethic.

As I mentioned previously, recommendations can also be posted in reference to educational experiences. I encourage you to search out these recommendations, especially if you are a younger business professional—and preferably before you graduate. Most professors consider it a privilege to assist a good student in securing his first job out of college.

One way to get recommendations is to give recommendations. If you write a recommendation for someone and she posts it to her profile, LinkedIn will automatically ask her if she would like to write a recommendation for you. I am not a fan of exchanging recommendations when it simply becomes friends endorsing friends. "He's a really good guy" is simply not a recommendation worth having, and sometimes these reciprocal recommendations consist of little more than that. However, if a recommendation exchange fits a specific need or situation, remind the person you are recommending that she could return the favor with her own detailed, specific, and strategic recommendation of you.

Prior to posting a recommendation to your profile, it is acceptable to suggest that the writer make revisions or corrections. LinkedIn gives you a chance to review a recommendation and send it back to the writer to request that any errors be corrected or additional details or keywords be added. Generally, the person who has written a recommendation for you will be more than happy to accommodate your suggestions.

Let me give you one final tip. If you want to have a great Monday morning, sit down on Sunday and write three or four recommendations for other people, totally out of the blue. If you do this, I am confident that no later than midmorning on Monday you will receive e-mails, phone calls, and comments through LinkedIn thanking you for writing a recommendation. People will say, "I can't believe you took the time to do that for me!" I have done this, and it works. The reason it sets you up for such a nice Monday morning is that it gives you a wave of confidence; you'll be ready to take on the day. Try it. You will have a lot of happy friends and connections going forward.

I want to close this chapter with a thought-provoking question: How would you feel if your competitors had more significant, specific recommendations on their profiles than you have on yours, and do you think those recommendations might make a difference as a potential customer or client reviews both of your profiles?

Case closed!

APPLYING THE POWER FORMULA

- You will be surprised by how much your **unique** connections would love to help you document and explain your **unique experience** by composing a well-written recommendation for you. Just ask!

- Differentiation from competitors is easy when you get a significant number of well-written recommendations.

- An added benefit of receiving recommendations is that the writer's 10-second bumper sticker appears on your profile. That sounds like a boost to your **unique experience** to me. And your 10-second bumper sticker will appear on the writer's profile—more great exposure for you.

CHAPTER 9

Not Your Average Joe

The LinkedIn Profile:
Professional Portfolio,
Special Sections, and Tools

Throughout the previous chapters on LinkedIn profiles, I have consistently emphasized the fact that one of the major purposes of your profile is to show credibility. Your profile and your actions on LinkedIn should establish you as an expert and prove that you are not your Average Joe. In this chapter you will learn how to make your profile unique and comprehensive by taking full advantage of your Professional Portfolio and other special profile sections. You will also see how use of the profile-reordering tool and strategic placement of calls to action can enhance your profile and produce business results.

Professional Portfolio

When it comes to enhancing your credibility, in my opinion this is the best feature on LinkedIn. You can share hyperlinks or upload various media, such as video, images, documents, and presentations. Most media file types are supported by this feature. You can place media or links in the Professional Portfolio area of your Summary, Experience, and Education profile sections.

Go to the specific profile section in which you'd like to add media and click the Add Media icon (see Figure 9.1). After you

Figure 9.1: Impress viewers of your profile by including your best presentations, customer testimonials, white papers, etc.

select the link box or "Upload a file" and link to or upload your media, a picture of your content will appear. The title and description fields will automatically fill with information from the web page or document, but you can change or delete this information if you prefer. If you follow these steps, your portfolio media or links will look similar to Figure 9.2.

Figure 9.2: A combination of interesting graphics and intriguing text will encourage readers to take action.

To get you thinking about how you might be able to use this feature, this is what I am currently sharing in my Professional Portfolio:

- My LinkedIn blog, where I share weekly LinkedIn tips and advice
- Promotional video for one of my live LinkedIn classes
- PowerPoint presentation of an infographic showing the results of my annual LinkedIn user survey
- Free download of a chapter from my book
- Video testimonial from a client praising the presentation I did for his organization
- Link to a sign-up form for my weekly LinkedIn tips and other LinkedIn information
- Link to my book page on Amazon.com
- Introductory video for a nonprofit organization (I serve on its board of directors)

I have generated a significant amount of business by including media and links on my profile. When I was a full-time office furniture guy, I had on my profile a document titled "Checklist for Moving Your Office." When I would meet a person at a networking event who was moving offices, right after I'd quit salivating about a potential sale, I'd hand him my business card and say, "Check out my LinkedIn profile—you'll find a checklist for moving your office. Print it off and give it to the person responsible for the move. He or she will simply love the checklist." This gives me immediate credibility and displays my expert status and my willingness to help. When that person goes home from the event and downloads the file, he will think, *Boy, Wayne has already added value in a brand new relationship. I think I'll continue this relationship and call him for help with the move and furniture for the new office.* Be creative, and share interesting material that will impress viewers of your profile and thereby increase your credibility. If you are a job seeker, this is a great place to put your resume (PDF format or video).

Additional Profile Sections

Whether you have a paid or free account, there are a number of special profile sections available to you. Including these sections in your LinkedIn profile will help you display your expertise, increase your credibility, and enhance your branding message. Currently the additional profile sections you can add are:

- Volunteering Experience
- Certifications
- Language
- Patents
- Publications
- Courses
- Honors & Awards
- Organizations

- Projects
- Test Scores
- Causes you care about
- Supported Organizations
- Personal Details

Right below your top box, you will see a list of available special sections (see Figure 9.3). Most of these are self-explanatory, and I suggest adding the ones that are applicable in your situation. If you speak multiple languages or hold a patent, let the world know about it. The Courses and Test Scores sections were obviously designed with students in mind, and this is an easy way for students to tout their academic work. It's all about differentiating yourself. Stand out from the crowd by adding these special sections and telling the world about your unique background or circumstances.

Figure 9.3: Set yourself apart from your competitors by including additional profile sections.

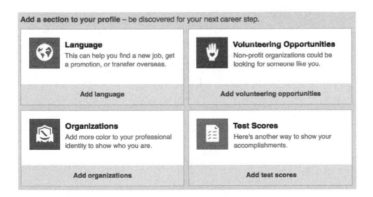

The following tips and strategies will help you take advantage of what I consider to be three of the most important special sections.

Skills & Endorsements

This section has gotten a lot of buzz because there is a lot more going on here than just a bunch of keywords that describe what you are good at. However, since you obviously want people to find you on LinkedIn, you should begin by including in this section words and/or phrases that describe who you are (experiences) and what you do (skill set). For example, I include terms like *LinkedIn trainer, LinkedIn consultant, LinkedIn keynote speaker, public speaking, social networking,* and *personal branding.* LinkedIn allows you to include up to fifty skills in this section of your profile. Obviously, the more terms you include, the more likely you will be found by people who are searching on LinkedIn.

An additional benefit of having skills on your profile is others can endorse you for those specific skills or expertise. Similar to "likes" on Facebook, everyone can see the number of endorsements you've received. In addition, the names and faces of the people who endorse you are displayed.

Here are a few facts, thoughts, and strategies relating to endorsements that will help you frame your approach to this important profile section:

- You can only receive endorsements from first-level connections and for skills you have acknowledged you possess.
- Don't feel obligated to endorse everyone who endorses you. Of course, if you can give a genuine endorsement of someone in your network, you should certainly return the favor.
- You control which endorsements are displayed on your profile. If you receive an endorsement from a person your network may view as not very credible, simply hide that endorsement.

- It's not necessary to thank everyone who endorses you. However, if you are looking to strengthen a relationship, by all means, send a note of thanks.
- LinkedIn's search ranking algorithm is top secret, but I suspect the number of endorsements on a profile is probably part of it. Thus, the more endorsements the better.
- Potential purchasers of your products and services can easily compare how many endorsements you have with how many your competitors have—another reason to actively seek endorsements.
- When you endorse someone, LinkedIn will notify her via e-mail, and your name and photo will appear on her profile. This is a great way to get her attention.

Endorsements are a great way to boost your credibility, so don't be bashful. Include a comprehensive list of your skills and expertise. Then get busy and request endorsements so the viewers of your profile can see just how good you are.

Volunteer Experience & Causes

This special section helps you tell the world what you care about and allows others to see a part of you that may not typically be available to the general public. Why is this important? Because it helps brand you as an individual who cares about your community and shows you leverage your time, talents, and treasures for the good of those in need. And as I mentioned previously, people love doing business with people who care about others.

The three categories in this section include "Causes you care about," "Organizations you support," and a place to describe in detail specific organizations and your role in those organizations

Figure 9.4: Help yourself and the charitable organizations you care about by including them on your profile.

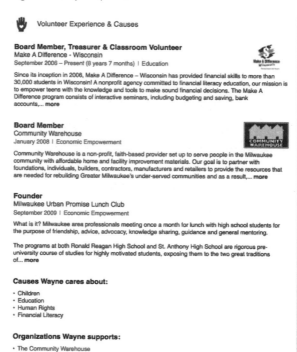

(see Figure 9.4). In addition to the personal benefit you derive from including this information on your LinkedIn profile, you are spreading your organization's message every time someone takes a look at your profile. It's great marketing for everyone, and—an added bonus—it's free!

Advice for Contacting [*insert your name*]

This optional section of your profile provides an opportunity to share your contact information with people outside of your first-level network. Because I prefer a very casual approach, I

Figure 9.5: You can provide contact information to make it easy for potential customers to inquire about your products and services.

Advice for Contacting Wayne

If you would like to chat about how I might be able to help you and/or your organization with all things LinkedIn feel free to contact me at wayne@powerformula.net or 414-313-7785. I hope to talk to you soon.

have personally chosen to include my phone number and e-mail address in narrative form (see Figure 9.5). Most salespeople I've encountered choose to openly share their phone number and e-mail address in this section. Some people choose to include a link to their website contact form. People who do not wish to share their contact information with the general public don't add this section to their profile. Only you can decide which approach is best for you.

Tools

In the remainder of this chapter, we're going to discuss two useful tools that will further enhance your profile: the section-relocating functionality and calls to action.

Reordering Your Profile Sections

The default order of your profile is top box, Summary, Experience, and so on. But because some readers may never read the middle or bottom portion of your profile, you may find it advantageous to place your most important information near the top. For example, if moving up your Experience section would tell your story more effectively—especially because you have some excellent information in your Professional Portfolio—do it. If you are a student who has little in the way of job experience but very substantial and impressive educational entries, you may want to move those entries up above your Summary section, or at least above your Experience section. Rearranging profile sections is easy—but keep in mind that not all profile sections can be moved. If a profile section is movable, you will see an up-down arrow to the right of the section heading. To move the entire Experience section, for instance, simply click the up-down arrow and drag the section to your desired location (see Figure 9.6). Also, if you'd like to move an individual entry within the Experience section,

Figure 9.6: Strategic placement of your profile components can greatly improve your effectiveness.

for instance, hover your cursor over the entry, and a gray vertical bar will appear to the left of the entry. Click the bar and then drag the entry to a new location.

Calls to Action

We have discussed the basics of creating an impressive LinkedIn profile. Now it's time to focus on precisely what you'd like readers of your profile to do after reading it. "That's simple," you say. "I want them to call me so we can do some business together!" But what if the reader is not quite ready to take that big step? What if he needs more information about you, your company, or your products/services before he picks up the phone or reaches out to you with an e-mail? This is where calls to action (CTAs) come in. What is a CTA? Wikipedia says this: "A call to action, or CTA, is a term used to describe a banner, button, or some type of graphic or text on a website meant to prompt a user to click it and continue down a conversion funnel."

Here are some actions you might call people to take when they review your LinkedIn profile:

- Download an informational document
- Watch a video
- Go to your website
- Listen to a podcast
- Read a product review
- Request a quote
- Read your blog

Your profile should have several CTAs to help move your reader down the conversion funnel and closer to that all-important step of contacting you. The best profile sections in which to include CTAs are:

- Headline
- Summary
- Websites
- Projects
- Publications
- Professional Portfolio
- Advice for Contacting [*your name is inserted here*]

For examples of the types of calls to action I have included on my LinkedIn profile, see Figure 9.2 on page 71 (Professional Portfolio) and Figure 9.7 (Summary section). To view all of my CTAs, check out my complete LinkedIn profile at www.linkedin.com /in/WayneBreitbarth.

Figure 9.7: Move your reader down the conversion funnel by offering valuable information.

My diverse business experience also allows me to share real-life stories and illustrations as I educate, motivate, and entertain audiences at national conventions, industry events, and conferences.

Check out my website at www.powerformula.net, where you can:

· sign up to receive my FREE weekly social media tips
· download lots of FREE social media resources
· view some of my video presentations
· read my blog
· learn about the many services I provide for individuals and companies

What good is a great-looking profile if it doesn't make you any money? Include some strategically placed calls to action on your LinkedIn profile, and then get ready for the customers to come knocking on your door.

Maximizing your use of the Professional Portfolio, additional profile sections, and tools discussed in this chapter will allow people to identify your areas of expertise and witness your desire to help others, which will significantly enhance your credibility. This is your chance to prove that you are *not* your Average Joe.

APPLYING THE POWER FORMULA

- How better to explain your **unique experience** than a PowerPoint presentation or video that positions you or your company as experts in your field?

- Be sure to use your Professional Portfolio for posting customer testimonials.

- LinkedIn offers a number of additional profile sections. Take advantage of this opportunity, and use any applicable special sections to showcase your **unique experience**.

- Placing calls to action throughout your profile will make it easy for viewers of your profile to get additional information about you and your company.

CHAPTER 10

Who Do You Want to Find?
Searching on LinkedIn

There are two major uses of LinkedIn, and we have spent a significant amount of time discussing the first use: being found. I have shown you how to develop a very beefy profile, which will allow you to be found based on keywords and the story you have told. In this chapter I will address the other major use of LinkedIn: finding others. LinkedIn can be used for finding not only prospective customers and clients but also for finding:

- New strategic vendor and supplier relationships
- People you want to join you in a project or endeavor, including a charity or not-for-profit with which you are involved
- New employees
- An expert in a specific industry
- Someone you want to engage in a social/business event (e.g., a golf outing or networking event)

- Strategic influencers of your customers and prospective customers
- People who manage important industry associations and organize events
- People you want to meet when you are out of town for an event
- A speaker for an upcoming event you are hosting

By using keywords and other search criteria—such as region, job title, group affiliation, etc.—you can easily find the people you are looking for. Ask yourself, *Who do I really want to find?* As a business owner, business developer, or job seeker, you will need to identify which keywords the person you want to find has most likely included in his profile. If that person has done a good job of creating his profile, it will include those keywords.

Bear in mind that by the time this book hits the shelves, LinkedIn will have around 400 million members. In other words, once you select your search criteria and hit the Search button, you are looking through what is the largest database of resumes in the world. No tool like this existed prior to LinkedIn, and the site becomes more and more useful each time a new person joins—and two people sign up every second of the day. As LinkedIn becomes increasingly popular, the database will become that much more useful. But enough of the generalities—let's get on to how an actual search might work.

My friends at M&M Office Interiors are always thinking about the keywords their potential customers would have in their profiles. Two of those words would be *facility* and *facilities*, because in many of the larger corporations the people they target have titles like Director of Facilities, Facility Manager, or something of a similar nature. The Advanced People Search function of LinkedIn is best for this type of searching. If you go to the top of any LinkedIn page, you can access this by clicking the word "Advanced," which is just to the right of the magnifying glass on the top right of the toolbar. I type "facility OR facilities" in the Title box (see Figure 10.1), check all four Relationship boxes (1st Connections, 2nd Connections, Group Members, and 3rd + Everyone

Figure 10:1: The Advanced People Search function enables you to perform very targeted searches.

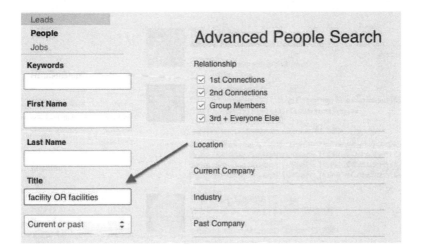

Else), and push the blue Search button (read more about the "or" search function on page 112). This searches the entire Linked-In network for my query, ultimately finding 288,619 profiles that have the word *facility* or *facilities* in their titles (see Figure 10.2). That's obviously too many to review, and M&M's market is not the entire world. So, if I go back and modify the advanced search to find contacts within a 50-mile radius of my zip code, I now get 2,766 results (see Figure 10.3). That number is more manageable and more regionally relevant, and if you think about what it represents—people in M&M's region who somewhere in their

Figure 10.2: A broad-ranging Advanced People Search may provide an impractical number of results.

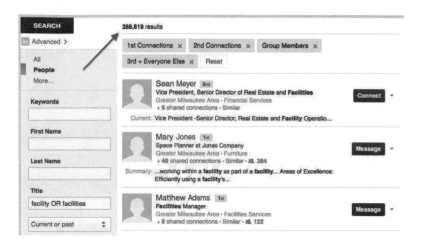

Figure 10.3: Add more specific criteria to narrow your search.

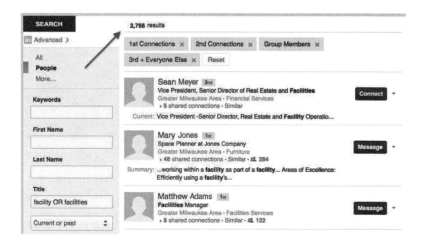

titles have the word *facility* or *facilities*—you see that this could be a very profitable list.

But let's continue refining the search before we look at the profiles. Let's say that, on top of *facility* or *facilities*, I would like to search for employees of a certain company. So, I choose one of the larger companies in the Milwaukee marketplace, Harley-Davidson, and add it to the Company box. Now I am searching for Harley-Davidson employees with *facility* or *facilities* in their titles who work at a location within 50 miles of my zip code. That produces 22 results (see Figure 10.4)

Figure 10.4: Further refine your search to uncover your perfect targets.

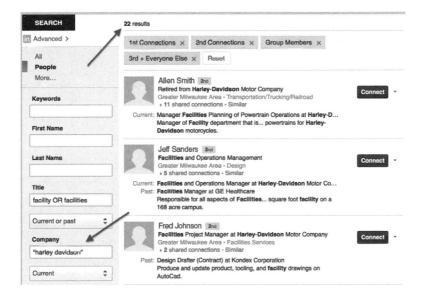

Now that you know how to use the different search boxes on the Advanced People Search page to narrow the entire LinkedIn database down to a small, targeted group, the world is your oyster. Don't limit yourself to simply searching for customers. When the development director of a local nonprofit organization (I serve on their board of directors) was in the process of applying for a grant, she searched for the foundation that was offering the grant. After she discovered I am connected to someone on the foundation's board, I called the board member and explained why this grant was so important to us. Our past applications had been unsuccessful, but this time—bingo—we received the grant, and it has been renewed multiple times since then. I'm confident you will find lots of ways to capitalize on this powerful LinkedIn feature, too.

I want to stop for a moment and talk about how the size of your network affects the results you receive when searching on LinkedIn. People come up to me regularly and say, "I've been to your class and I can't get LinkedIn to work. I'm just not finding anyone." The first question I ask them is "How many connections do you have?" When they proudly tell me they have 35 connections, I tell them they are fishing for muskie with a minnow net.

I am an avid fisherman, and in Wisconsin the grandpappy of all game fish is the muskie. When my wife and I are fishing for muskie, we place a huge net in the middle of the boat, always ready to net "the big one" once we get it close enough to the boat. You need that huge net if you want to catch a trophy-size muskie. The LinkedIn equivalent of the muskie net is a significant number of connections. There is no exact number you must have to perform effective searches, but I do know it takes at least 75 to 100 quality connections before your search will consistently "net" you significant results (no pun intended!).

Let's go back to the Harley-Davidson example for a moment. If you live in Milwaukee and have 50 connections, your competitor has 500 connections, and you both conduct the same search for facilities people at Harley, each of you should get 22 search results. There are 22 people on LinkedIn who meet those specific criteria. The difference will be the amount of profile information you can see for each of those 22 people. Currently, for instance, with a free LinkedIn account, you can see full profiles of first-, second-, and third-level connections. For people who belong to a group to which you also belong, you will see their first name and last initial and limited profile information. If you have no connection to a person, you will see a generic description; for example, "Linked-In member, BA Marquette University 1999, Milwaukee, WI, Automotive"—which is obviously not very useful. However, please note that LinkedIn changes the rules quite frequently in regard to what you are allowed to see, and thus as you read this book, you may be able to see more or less than I've just enumerated.

What does this mean for you versus your competitor? Well, with 500 connections, she is probably more closely connected to these 22 people than you are, and thus she will be able to see more useful information than you will see. However, there's always the chance it could be your lucky day, and one of your 50 connections is a close relative of the vice president of facilities at Harley. But since that's pretty unlikely, your best options are growing your network or upgrading your LinkedIn account, because with a paid account you could see full profiles of the 22 people.

This part of LinkedIn, the finding part, really rewards the person who has spent time building his flat network and then makes the effort to put those people into LinkedIn as first-level connections. As discussed earlier in the book, the ongoing process of adding connections will always pay off; each time you add a Number 1, you are adding Number 2's and Number 3's who might be able to help you accomplish your goals. However, do not lose sight of the fact that I am still talking about having a quality network of trusted professionals. If you choose to lower the quality bar and connect with very casual acquaintances and/or strangers, the likelihood your connection will be able to introduce you to the person you really want to meet is greatly diminished.

Saved Searches

Once you land on a search that produces quality targets for you, LinkedIn allows you to save that search. This is one of the best features on LinkedIn, but it is often overlooked. From the screen that shows your search results, simply click "Save search" on the top right and then choose whether you want LinkedIn to send you an e-mail weekly or monthly to notify you if a new person who meets your search criteria has been found in your network. You can save up to three searches with a free LinkedIn account.

If you are not saying to yourself, *Oh my gosh, that is so cool!* you are not understanding the power of the Saved Search function. This is a perpetual lead generator, and it is absolutely free. So, when LinkedIn notifies you of a new search result, get on the phone and set up a meeting with this person who has become a part of your network. It could turn out to be a home run.

In response to the user surveys I conduct on an annual basis, Advanced People Search is consistently rated as one of the most useful features on LinkedIn. This is really where the money is. It's where you will undoubtedly see the majority of your productivity on LinkedIn. Once your network has grown to "muskie size" and you have learned how to maximize your search results, you should begin to see an even greater return on your time investment in LinkedIn. Using the all-important keywords, consistently try to identify and search for the person you would love to find and make a connection with—and then get the net ready.

APPLYING THE POWER FORMULA

- The winner in the searching part of the LinkedIn game is generally the person who has the most **unique relationships** (in other words, connections). It's as simple as that.

- Saved searches is your way of making sure LinkedIn is looking for your future **unique relationships** 24/7, even when you are sleeping, on vacation, or hanging out with friends.

Develop a winning strategy to find the "right" people with the worksheet "LinkedIn People Searching: Your Ticket to Improved ROI," available on page 197.

CHAPTER 11

I Found You—Now What Do I Do with You?

Contacting the Person You Just Found

You will remember we found a list of facilities people at Harley-Davidson in the Milwaukee area that consisted of 22 connections. Figure 11.1 shows the names of some of those people. Now you need to review the profile of each individual and make sure that person is someone you would actually like to meet. If you decide to proceed at this point using the good old-fashioned business techniques we have used for years, like picking up the phone, e-mailing, etc., at least you now know the name of the person and are not simply cold-calling Harley-Davidson and asking for the facilities person. But if you have no success with the traditional methods, you can pull up his LinkedIn profile and scroll down the right-hand side, where you'll see who in your network knows that person (see Figure 11.2).

Figure 11.1: Narrow your search further by reviewing profiles.

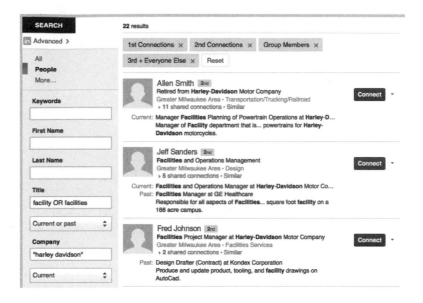

Figure 11.2: The invisible has just become visible.

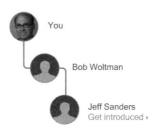

This is where you could pick up the phone, call your friend, and ask how strong a relationship he has with the person at Harley. If your friend's network is made up of trusted professionals, you could request that he make an introduction or pass along a message to the Harley employee to give your efforts to connect with that person a bit of a push. Isn't this what people in your network have always done for you? The difference with LinkedIn is you can now know who knows whom by simply pushing the Search button. As I stated earlier, this is one of the great powers of LinkedIn; it makes connections that are normally invisible visible.

The Introduction Function

LinkedIn's Introduction function can help you get introduced to second-level connections. This tool allows you to draft a LinkedIn message to your first-level connection, asking him to introduce you to one of his first-level connections whom you'd like to meet. You can access the Introduction function in one of two ways. From the search screen, you can click "Get Introduced" when you see someone you want to meet (see Figure 11.3). If you are viewing the person's profile, you can click "Get introduced" (see Figure 11.4).

Figure 11.3: Initiate an introduction via LinkedIn.

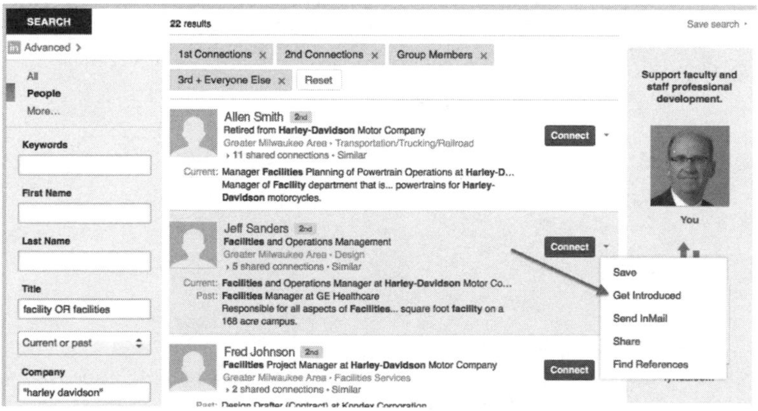

Figure 11.4: Get introduced after viewing an intriguing profile.

If you click on "Get Introduced" and you are connected to your ultimate target through more than one person, you will need to select which of your first-level connections you feel will be in a better position to help you. Once you select that first-level connection, you will then get a screen that looks like Figure 11.5.

Figure 11.5: Your connection's endorsement may open the door.

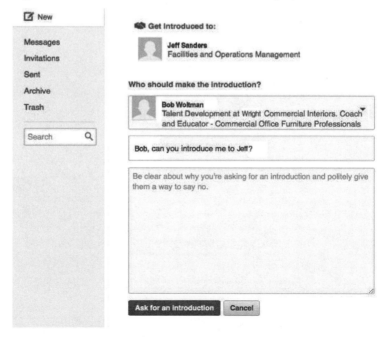

There will be two boxes—one for the subject of your message and one for enumerating why you want to get introduced to his connection. Simply explain your business proposition and why you would like to meet, no differently than if you were picking up the phone. Be sure to start with a personal greeting, and then ask him if he would pass the introduction along through LinkedIn.

When you push the "Ask for an Introduction" button, the message goes to your trusted connection, and this is where some of the power of LinkedIn comes in. Your connection will then have an opportunity to write something nice about you, maybe even about the project or product you talked about in the message, and reaffirm that you are a good person to work with. Then, when he pushes "Send Message," that information goes on to the person you wish to meet.

The very first time you attempt to use the Introduction function, it may feel a little odd, since most of us did not grow up connecting through the Internet and social media. We grew up using things like the telephone, regular mail, and, most recently, e-mail for making connections like this. But soon I suspect the Facebook generation will see social media as the primary way to connect with people. And since they are an integral part of the business community, it behooves the rest of the business world to engage with them in this way.

Even if you are comfortable with meeting a new contact through LinkedIn, you should make sure your friend understands how the Introduction function works and what his role in the process is. With a free LinkedIn account, you can have only five outstanding introductions at any given point in time, so you want to be sure that none of them gets stuck with someone who is unfamiliar with LinkedIn introductions. If your friend hasn't passed on the introduction after several days, you may want to call him up and explain the process.

In my opinion, using the Introduction function on LinkedIn is a more respectful and potentially more effective way to ask for an introduction than using the telephone. With the Introduction tool, your connection gets a chance to review your message when he has sufficient time to do so; you don't have to tie him down and ask for an introduction while he is busy trying to get work done. He also gets the chance to write a detailed recommendation about you to pass along to his friend, and if he does so, the connection is much more likely to take place. For these reasons, I think LinkedIn's Introduction feature will be a tool that many people will come to use more frequently, especially as more members of the Facebook generation join the workforce.

No matter which technique you decide to use—phone, snail mail, e-mail, face-to-face, or the LinkedIn Introduction tool—the information you receive after doing an advanced LinkedIn search will help you get to the person you want to meet much faster and more effectively than any tool we've had up to this point in our business careers.

APPLYING THE POWER FORMULA

- When you are writing a message to your first-level connection requesting an introduction to his/her first-level connection, be sure to highlight or reaffirm your **unique experience** and explain how that experience will help your target accomplish his/her goals.

- If you are the individual passing along the introduction to a connection, help your friend out by saying something nice about him and his capabilities so that your connection is encouraged to reach out.

CHAPTER 12

There's Gold in Them Thar Hills

Expanding Your Network

As you can tell from previous chapters, the winner of the searching aspect of the LinkedIn game is generally the person who has a lot of connections. However, please continue to keep in mind my recommendation that you only add to your network people whom you know and trust, because when you add a new contact, you put your extremely valuable network in his or her hands. Remember, it is **your** network. It is a possession you have worked your entire career to build, and when you add a connection on LinkedIn, it is like handing your Outlook database to that individual and trusting him to treat it professionally as you would treat his.

I recommend you have an ultimate goal of acquiring at least 200 to 250 connections (muskie size), as opposed to the 50 or 60 connections (minnow size) the vast majority of LinkedIn users acquire. If you want your searches to be useful, you really want to consistently add connections. This chapter will show you how to find new people to add, accept or decline the requests you'll get, and gather interesting information about your expanding base of contacts. Once you've built your muskie-sized net, when you go fishing you'll be sure to come up with lots of potentially valuable connections.

The most common way to add connections is one at a time. You do this by clicking "Add Connections" on the top toolbar under the Connections heading. Then select "Any Email" and choose "Invite by individual email" (see Figure 12.1). All you need is the person's e-mail address, and then you can use Linked-In's standard invitation to invite your friend or colleague to join your network.

Figure 12.1: Adding connections one at a time is as easy as 1-2-3.

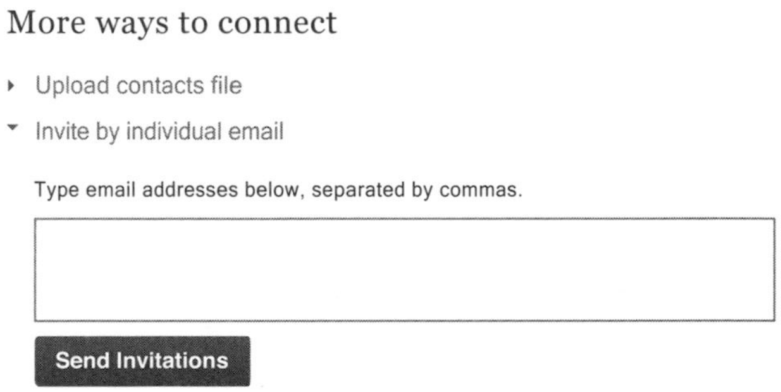

More ways to connect

‣ Upload contacts file

▾ Invite by individual email

Type email addresses below, separated by commas.

Send Invitations

The preferable way, however, to add a person to your network is to search for her by name, go to her profile, and then click the big blue Connect button. Once you make this selection, you must then tell LinkedIn and the person how you know her by selecting one of the options LinkedIn shows you: colleague, classmate, etc. I prefer this method of adding connections rather than the option mentioned in the previous paragraph because it allows you to enter a short personal note explaining why it would be beneficial for the person to allow you to be part of her network. In my opinion, the standard "I'd like to add you to my professional network on LinkedIn" is very lame. Remember, you are adding this person to your group of trusted professionals. Therefore, you should add a personal touch to your invitation, and customizing the connection request will get you a much higher response rate.

Here are seven simple suggestions for creating what I like to refer to as a five-star connection request. There is a 300-character limit for your personal message, but that should be more than enough to get your relationship started on the right foot.

1. Use the person's name in your greeting.
2. Mention where you met him/her (in person, on the phone, online) and/or who you have in common.
3. Suggest a face-to-face or phone meeting if you want to develop a deeper relationship with the person.
4. Offer something of value based on your review of the person's profile or your personal knowledge of the individual.
5. Explain how you can help the person or how he/she could help you.
6. Help the person feel good about the connection. I usually say, "I would be honored to have you join my LinkedIn network."
7. Include a friendly closing statement. "Sincerely" is a little bit stiff in most circumstances. For instance, I might say "Go Pack Go" to a fellow Wisconsinite.

Of course, you won't be able to include all seven suggestions in every invitation, but choose the most relevant ones in each situation. If you follow these simple suggestions, more people will accept your invitations, and your new relationships will be off to a strong start.

Finding valuable people whom you can invite to join your network can be challenging, but LinkedIn has some great features to help you quickly grow your network. Not only is it easy to find former classmates and coworkers, but LinkedIn also shows you who has taken a look at your profile and thus might be interested in joining your network or doing business with you.

Connecting with Classmates

The first step, connection with classmates, is fun—it will feel like you're on Facebook. To access the Alumni feature, click "Find Alumni" under the Connections tab on the top toolbar. This will take you to the University page of one of the schools you attended. If you click the blue Change University box on the right, you can pick a different school. LinkedIn will give you a list of all the LinkedIn members who have said they attended this school. You can filter the list by where they live, where they work, what they do, what they studied, what skills they possess, and how you're connected to them. By clicking any of the composite results (city, company name, skill, etc.), you will narrow the search, and you'll then see the people who meet your search criteria (see Figure 12.2).

The exercise above will undoubtedly result in quite a large number of potential connections, but if you say to yourself, *Well, that's too many; that's going to take me too long to review*, then I guess you don't really understand why you are even on LinkedIn. Rather than viewing this process as a hassle, treat your search for valuable connections as if you were hunting treasure—tell yourself, *There's gold in them thar hills.* Your classmates present a tremendous opportunity to make some important connections. These are people who

Figure 12.2: Strengthen your network by adding fellow alumni from your college or university.

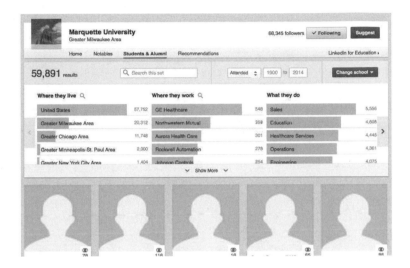

will remember you from your college days, and you will now be able to tell them what you are up to today. Reconnecting with old friends is fun, but it can also be very productive; some of your old drinking buddies may now be presidents of the companies with which you are trying to do business. Many others will likely have nice databases of Number 1 connections, which could lead to great connections at the second or third level for you. You just never know.

"People You May Know"

If you hover over the Add Connections icon on your LinkedIn toolbar, you will see a list of people you may know (see Figure 12.3). LinkedIn has a special formula for putting people in this section, and although they have not revealed how it works, you will be amazed at the names you find here. From

Figure 12.3: LinkedIn helps you find new connections.

my observation, these people typically fall into one or more of the following categories:

- They are connected to someone in your network.
- They attended a school that you also attended.
- They are a member of a group to which you belong.

You will find these suggestions not only useful but also somewhat entertaining. LinkedIn has helped me find a number of guys I used to drink dime taps (10¢ beers) with during my college days! Do not overlook the usefulness of this feature in finding new connections.

"Who's Viewed Your Profile?"

LinkedIn also allows users to see how many people are looking at their profile with the "Who's Viewed Your Profile?" feature,

Figure 12.4: More looks at your profile should create more business opportunities.

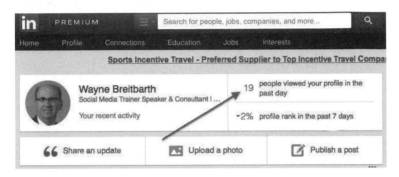

which you'll find on the top of your LinkedIn home page (see Figure 12.4). This is an interesting box to click on from time to time, but don't expect to always see the name of the person who looked at your profile. You may instead see any of the following information about the person: job title, type of company or industry, company name, location, or simply "LinkedIn member." From this information, you can sometimes guess who viewed your profile and perhaps may be interested in meeting you. The person who is "checking you out" chooses whether you will be able to see his/her name or not. In Chapter 17, I will discuss this and other settings that are available for each individual LinkedIn user.

The "Who's Viewed Your Profile?" section can also help you identify whether you are increasing your activity and presence on LinkedIn. It will display information like "Your profile has been viewed by 27 people in the last 3 days." You can also see how you rank for profile views among your connections. As with all networking, increasing your activity has the potential to increase relationships, which may lead to increased business.

Accepting or Declining Connection Requests

People frequently ask me what they should do when somebody they don't know invites them to connect on LinkedIn. This will begin to happen with greater frequency as you become more active on LinkedIn, especially if you decide to join larger groups. Some people assume that because you are members of the same group, you will want to connect with them on the first-degree level.

Figure 12.5: Consider all of your options when responding to an invitation.

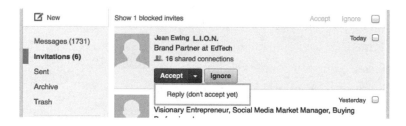

When you receive an invitation from someone, you will see the screen in Figure 12.5. Let's go through the three options you have when responding to an invitation:

1. **Accept**. The person will immediately become a first-degree connection.

2. **Reply (don't accept yet)**. People often overlook the option of using the Reply feature because it is not readily visible as an option. If you click the down arrow next to the word "Accept," you will see this option: "Reply (don't accept yet)." When you choose this option, you can send

a communication to the requesting individual without allowing him to become part of your network. If I have had an interesting meeting with a person and we belong to the same group or club, I can send a message saying something like, "At the next meeting, let's make sure we connect and get to know each other better so we can join each other's LinkedIn network."

3. **Ignore**. The invitation will be put into the archive file and marked "Ignore." Before deciding to ignore an invitation, I suggest you check out the person's profile to determine whether there might be a reason to meet him or her.

   After selecting "Ignore," you will have two additional options—"I don't know [*name*]" or "This is spam." If you select "I don't know [*name*]," the person will not be allowed to send you any more invitations. In both instances your feedback assists LinkedIn in deciding whether to restrict this person's account in some way.

Connecting with Competitors

One question that comes up quite frequently is, "Would you let competitors be connected to you at the first level?" My immediate response is "No!" It does not make good business sense to allow your competitors to have a list of the people who are most important to you. You are basically handing them your Outlook database. There are, however, certain industries in which your competitors may also be your suppliers or vendors, and you will need to weigh the risk and reward of allowing those individuals to be part of your network.

Tags

Once you've got all these connections, you'll want to use tags to sort them for easy reference. LinkedIn defines tags as "simple keywords that you can create to organize your connections for quick filtering on LinkedIn." You can create up to 200 unique tags. To use this feature, go to the profile of any one of your first-level connections, select the Relationship tab, click "Tag," and then follow the prompt (see Figure 12.6). Examples of tags I have found useful include "bankers," "insurance agents," and "customers."

Figure 12.6: Use tags to organize and target groups of people with similar characteristics.

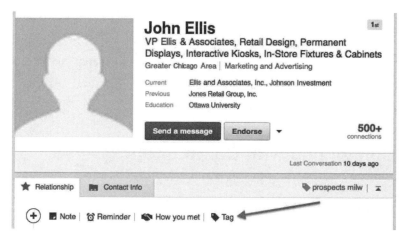

After you apply your desired tags to the people in your network, you can begin sorting by tag. For instance, if I am hosting a webinar for accountants, I will search for everyone in my network who has my "accountant" tag. I can then send a direct message with details about the webinar to 50 accountants at a time. As you spend time using this feature, you will find more ways to use tags to help you organize your network, which can save you time when you need to locate or contact a particular person or group within your network.

Taking advantage of the features explained in this chapter will enable you to quickly add a large number of connections. You'll be on your way to building that big muskie net, so that when you search for new contacts, you will have plenty of people to choose from.

APPLYING THE POWER FORMULA

- Making connections using the steps outlined in this chapter may take you six to eight hours to complete, but it's well worth the effort. Every one of your **unique relationships** gives you lots of Number 2's and 3's, and any of them could be the person you want to meet.

- These steps work more effectively when you have thoroughly outlined your **unique experience** in the Experience and Education sections. If you fail to list a job or an educational experience, you will miss out on potential credibility as well as the opportunity to make valuable connections with people you met while gaining that **unique experience**.

Identify the connection strategy that will help you grow your business and brand by downloading "The LinkedIn Connection Conundrum: Who Should Be in Your Network?" available at **www.powerformula.net/connections**.

CHAPTER 13

Keywords Are King

Maximizing Your Ability to Find and Be Found by Others

By this time you are probably tired of me talking about the importance of keywords. However, when I teach my classes, I find that many people are not well versed on the logic and rules of keywords and searching.

You have invested a lot of time and effort in creating a perfect profile and building your list of connections, so that when you pull out the muskie net, you can expect to catch lots of potential customers, job candidates, new vendors, etc. Understanding the rules presented in this chapter will help you maximize your effectiveness on LinkedIn by giving you much stronger search results.

Searching on LinkedIn works in much the same way as searching elsewhere on the Internet; it is based on Boolean logic. Here are a few of the basic rules of Boolean logic and examples of how you can use them effectively.

Exact Phrases

If you are looking for a specific group of words in a certain order, put that group of words in quotation marks. For example, the search term **interior design** should be put in quotes; otherwise you will get results that include pages where **interior** and **design** show up separately rather than pages where the phrase **interior design** appears.

The "And" Function

Placing the upper-case word **AND** or the plus sign (+) between search terms shows you search results that contain all of the words or phrases you entered. For example, if I am looking for someone who has both **office furniture** and **interior design** in her profile, I would type in either **"office furniture"** AND **"interior design"** or **"office furniture"** + **"interior design."** However, you can leave the "AND" or plus sign out, and LinkedIn will assume there is an "AND" between the two terms (in other words, **"office furniture"** **"interior design"** would yield the same result as the other searches).

The "Or" Function

Placing an upper-case **OR** between search terms shows you results that contain any one of the search terms but not necessarily both. A search for **CPA OR owner** would give you results for all people who have either the word **CPA** or **owner** somewhere in their profile.

The "Not" Function

Placing the minus sign (-) or the word **NOT** in all caps before a search term excludes that term from the results. For example, if you were looking for someone who is in sales but not in marketing, you would type in **sales NOT marketing** or **sales - marketing**, which will show you profiles that contain the word **sales** but not the word **marketing**.

There are many articles on the Internet that discuss further principles of Boolean logic; you can find them through a quick search. Most of us who spend time developing our LinkedIn networks expect a return on our investment, and becoming proficient at keyword searching is one of the most important steps toward realizing that goal.

Keyword Optimizing Your Profile

Now let's discuss your own keywords and the steps that will help ensure you're near the top of the list when people search LinkedIn for keywords related to what you do. Improving your ranking is very similar to the work that search engine optimization companies do in order to move business websites up in the search results on Google. If you are a business owner with a website, you probably paid lots of money to have your website optimized for keyword searching. Your LinkedIn profile is your personal website, and this is your chance to keyword optimize your profile—without having to pay tons of money to an SEO expert. Follow these steps:

1. Go to the Advanced People Search function (discussed in Chapter 10) and put your most important keywords in the Keyword box and check all four Relationship boxes (see Figure 13.1). For example, let's use the phrase "office furniture." If you serve a certain region of the country, select the radius and zip code that best covers your market (see Figure 13.2). Once you hit the blue Search button, scroll through the search results and note exactly where your

Figure 13.1: Start the process of keyword optimizing your profile.

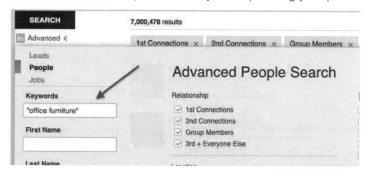

Figure 13.2: Carefully defining your market will result in more meaningful search results.

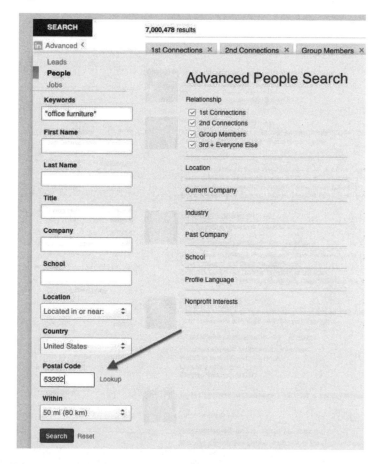

profile shows up. If it's not on the first page, you have some work to do—but even if it does show up on the first page, your goal should be to become the first search result in your region for that keyword or set of keywords.

2. Revise your profile, adding the top keywords you identified in step 1 to any and all of the following five areas: Headline, Summary, Skills, Experience Title, and Experience Description. Based on the blogs I have read, you get extra LinkedIn search weighting by having these words in your headline, experience titles, and Skills section, and my research backs up that claim. Also try to get these keywords dropped into any new recommendations you receive.

In my situation, I might be tempted to simply list "LinkedIn Trainer, LinkedIn Trainer, LinkedIn Trainer" wherever I can, but remember that you want your profile to be understandable and readable. Therefore, do your best to incorporate the keywords naturally. Once you have added additional keywords to your profile, perform the same search and see if you have moved up in the results.

When I owned M&M Office Interiors, I prided myself on being the number-one hit when I'd search for office furniture in the Milwaukee area. There were times when I lost that position and had to work very hard to move myself back to the top. Now that I spend the majority of my time helping companies use LinkedIn to increase sales and raise brand awareness, it is even more challenging to stay at the top of the search rankings. Why? Because my competitors are all LinkedIn experts who are constantly looking for new ways to be number one in the search rankings!

When I started working with the ten-person sales team of a manufacturing company, the highest search ranking for any of the ten people was page 8. After brainstorming with them about their business and strategically optimizing their profiles, eight of the ten salespeople began appearing on page 1. Needless to say, this made for a very happy client.

Keywords are your ticket to finding your target audience and getting noticed by the people who can help you reach your goals. Apply Boolean logic when using keywords to search for others, and be diligent in continuing to add keywords to your profile to improve your search ranking—you want to be at the top of the list, where people will notice you.

APPLYING THE POWER FORMULA

- Keywords are king. Combinations of keywords are the king and his court. Be sure to look at your competitors' profiles in detail and scout out what words they use to explain their **unique experience**. You may find some you have missed.

- You may want to survey some of your best customers and ask them, "If you were to search for me or my company on the Internet, what words would you use?" Use these **unique relationships** and your ability to ask them these types of questions to your advantage.

Rank higher in LinkedIn search results with the help of this handy worksheet, "Keywords: The Key to Being Found on LinkedIn," available on page 201.

CHAPTER 14

How Do Companies Fit into the LinkedIn Landscape?

Researching Companies on LinkedIn and Other Company-Related Matters

One very useful function of LinkedIn is the ability to learn more about companies. Rumor has it that company pages may become one of the exclusive benefits of paid LinkedIn accounts, but at the present time it is still free—and very powerful. Also, since LinkedIn went public, they appear to be spending a lot of their marketing efforts on opportunities and products for companies. By the time this book hits the shelves, I expect there will be many updates and changes. Visit my website at www.powerformula. net, and register to receive updates to this book as well as weekly LinkedIn tips and information about newly released features.

To search for companies on LinkedIn, click the arrow to the left of the Search box at the top of any LinkedIn page (see Figure 14.1). Select "Companies" from the drop-down menu, and use

Figure 14.1: LinkedIn makes it easy to find companies that meet your criteria.

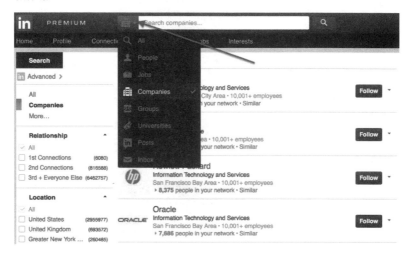

keywords, company name, location, etc. to search for relevant companies. When you click on a company in the search results, you will get what LinkedIn refers to as a company page. Currently there are more than 7 million LinkedIn company pages. There is a lot of useful information contained on company pages, and the LinkedIn company database is growing rapidly. In fact, many people consider it more useful than Hoover's, which a lot of us access on a fee basis.

On the top of a company's page, you will see general company information, including the company's Specialties section. As we discussed with regard to the Specialties section of an individual's profile, placement of relevant keywords in this section will greatly enhance a company's ability to be found in LinkedIn user searches.

The list below is certainly not an exhaustive catalog of the information available on a company's LinkedIn page, but these are some of the items I have found useful—particularly when searching for potential customers and new employees as well as attempting to stay on top of what my competitors are doing.

- A list of all company employees who are in your network
- The total number of employees who have LinkedIn accounts
- Company-generated status updates
- A list of the company's current job postings on Linked-In, accessed by clicking the Careers tab at the top of the company page
- The company's LinkedIn Showcase pages (listed in the right-hand column), which highlight various products, services, and markets they serve

When you have identified a company or organization in which you have an ongoing interest, LinkedIn gives you the opportunity to receive notification of any changes to that company's profile page. This can be done by clicking the yellow Follow box on the top right side of the page. You will then receive notification of any changes to the page as part of your network updates. This form of "stalking" is an effective way to keep track of your targets, which could include current and prospective customers, competitors, or organizations with which you are seeking employment.

You have already discovered the many benefits of searching for people on LinkedIn, and searching for companies can be equally beneficial. I've already shown you how to do a basic company search, but your search will undoubtedly be more useful if you narrow the parameters. Let's say you want to find an office furniture dealership in your area but also want to be sure the dealership can provide interior design services. You would enter "office furniture" and "interior design" in the Search Companies box. Once the results are displayed, you will be able to regional-ize your search or enter a specific location (see Figure 14.2). You can also modify your search by:

- Industry
- Company size
- Number of company followers
- Relationship (three options available: 1st degree, 2nd degree, 3rd degree + everyone else)
- Companies that have jobs posted on LinkedIn
- Company's Fortune 1000 ranking

Figure 14.2: A laser-focused search can produce an extremely relevant list of companies.

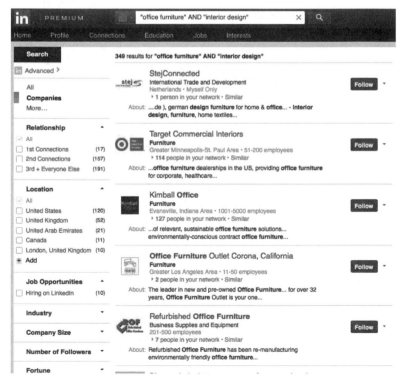

If you are the person responsible for setting up your company page on LinkedIn, you can get started by clicking "Companies" under the Interests tab on your top toolbar and then clicking the yellow "Create" button. You can then enter whatever basic organizational information your company wants to share with the LinkedIn community and the entire Google world. Your company's LinkedIn page will show up when someone searches for your company using Google, and many times it will be near the top of the list. Be sure to carefully draft your company's LinkedIn page so that its story is presented in a very positive and professional manner.

Social Media Policies and Procedures

Social media is creating many great business development opportunities, not only for individuals but for companies as well. If you are a company leader or the person responsible for organizational policies and procedures, you will need to decide whether your company will embrace these new social media tools and—if so—how you will develop a set of effective company policies relating to them. No one wants more policies, but what can be a great tool can also be a great detriment to the business if used improperly.

In the classes I lead, questions about companies and social media come up more and more, and it is very important to think about the following items as you draft your company's official position on LinkedIn:

1. What rules do you want to have about LinkedIn usage on company time?

2. What branding message do you want shared with the public—not only on the company page but also on each individual profile page that mentions your company?

3. What keywords and descriptions of your company do you want included in your employees' profiles?
4. Will you allow employees to receive recommendations from and write recommendations for your clients or customers?
5. Will you allow employees to write recommendations for each other?

Considering these questions may make you doubt that you should even play the social media game. But do not be discouraged. More and more companies are gaining market share by effectively using social media to communicate with customers, employees, and business partners, and you do not want to be left behind. It's just a matter of taking the lead and having enough knowledge to feel comfortable with your company's presence in this sphere.

Get started by bringing together a group of people to discuss how you can consistently brand your company using tools like LinkedIn, Facebook, Twitter, and others. Discuss your strategy for communicating via social media because your company's message can become inconsistent when each individual employee uses his or her own style to present information about the organization. Although LinkedIn and other social media sites are designed to be about individuals rather than companies, your efforts to strategize with a committee of your employees and colleagues will help your company have a stronger and more consistent online presence.

You will find that individuals from the Facebook generation will be very excited to give input. They tend to love social networking tools, to the point that many do not even regard it as work. In contrast, many of us from non-Facebook generations find social networking frustrating and time-consuming, and we may not understand the results that our efforts can produce. The committee you put together should consist of people who are willing to lead the charge and who actually enjoy being involved in high-level strategy sessions about branding and marketing for the company.

APPLYING THE POWER FORMULA

- Nothing benefits your company's search rankings more than you and all your employees having lots of first-degree connections. This is yet another way those **unique relationships** pay off.

- You may have already optimized your company website with certain keywords. Be sure to put these same keywords in the Specialties section of your LinkedIn company page.

- Do not underestimate the power of telling your company's **unique** story in the Description section of the company page. This may be the only bit of information a person sees before contacting you. Think of it as a free listing in a 400-million-person searchable database. Now that's power.

LinkedIn is a sure-fire way to grow your company's market share and increase revenue. But are you making costly mistakes? Download "10 LinkedIn Mistakes Companies Make—and How to Fix Them Before They Damage Your Company's Reputation" at **www.powerformula.net/mistakes** to learn more.

CHAPTER 15

Revving Up Your LinkedIn Efforts by Joining Groups
The Power of LinkedIn Groups

Social networking is all about people coming together, sharing information, and forming communities, and LinkedIn is no exception. The Groups feature on LinkedIn is one of the most effective tools on the site for interacting with people in your industry, region, or specialty. Participants in my annual LinkedIn user survey consistently rate groups and people searching as the most important features on the site.

Groups are very easy to join, and you can belong to as many as fifty at any time. I recommend joining close to that amount. Here are some of the most compelling reasons to join groups:

1. You will be found.
2. You will find others who have similar affiliations or interests.

3. Joining groups in which your customers, suppliers, or vendors hang out is a way to connect, answer questions, and share resources, expertise, and events.

4. You will find job opportunities, because every group has job postings and job discussions.

5. You can become a credible expert by answering questions and posting articles of interest for the entire group to see.

6. In groups, people talk about events they are involved in, and this may help you find activities of interest to you.

7. You can promote an event you are hosting to a group of people who have the same interests.

8. You can search within groups and communicate with members to whom you are not officially connected.

Let me give you an example of this last benefit because it is not always appreciated or understood. If you look at the group Link Up Milwaukee (see Figure 15.1), with 17,515 members, it is the largest group in the region. The larger the group, the larger the

Figure 15.1: Take advantage of the searching power large groups can provide.

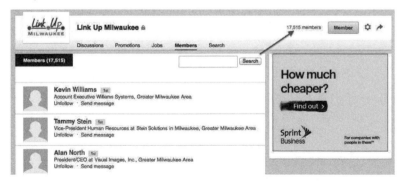

pool of LinkedIn members available for you to search for high-value contacts. Searching groups is a very powerful tool in building your muskie net; being a member of Link Up Milwaukee allows me to keyword search those 17,515 members for people I want to meet—whether directly or through a mutual connection. And because I am a member of Link Up Milwaukee, I can send direct messages to all my fellow group members, although I cannot look at their connections and don't have the other privileges of a Number 1 connection.

Groups like this one present yet another opportunity for connection with people beyond the traditional phone call, e-mail, or snail mail. However, even though I think groups are very valuable, I am not a fan of asking people to join your network simply because you belong to the same LinkedIn group. You will get invitations like that, but remember—for most people it is advisable to connect only with people you know and trust.

As I mentioned earlier, you should try to join fifty groups. The reason I suggest joining this many is because different types of groups have different purposes. We have already addressed the benefits of very large groups. Then you have groups in your specific industry. You will want to join national, regional, and local groups that focus on your particular specialty. For example, if you are an accountant, you may want to join the CPA & Business Professional Group, which is a national group with more than 50,000 members. This will allow you to find information about national events, educational opportunities, and industry trends. If your accounting practice is in Wisconsin, you could join WICPA (Wisconsin Institute of CPAs), which has more than 2,700 members and would give you access to regional information, such as proposed statewide legislation related to accounting issues.

Locally, you could join the Milwaukee & Waukesha Area Accounting Professionals group, which includes more than 850 accounting professionals who share ideas and job leads. If your firm specializes in accounting for nonprofits, joining NonProfit MidWest (450+ members) would give you an opportunity to identify potential clients who do business in your geographic region. The fifty groups you join will depend on your strategy, what your products or services are, and where you provide those products or services.

The types of groups you should join are:

- "Birds of a feather" groups—alumni associations, chambers, clubs, religious organizations, hobby groups, etc.
- Industry groups (both inside and outside of your region)
- LinkedIn or other social media user groups (These groups concentrate on helping each other be more productive on these sites.)
- Regional super groups (like Link Up Milwaukee)

Once you join a large number of communities, you may want to turn off the e-mail notifications for discussions taking place in some of the larger groups—the ones you may have joined solely because of the size of their memberships. Many times the topics being discussed in these large groups will not be of interest to you. For instance, in Wisconsin, a popular group to join is the Green Bay Packers Fans group. With over 7,900 members, it gives you lots of searching power. However, when I joined, I promptly turned off the e-mail notifications because I wasn't interested in the constant Brett Favre banter. You can turn off e-mail notifications by changing the settings in the individual group's Settings section (see Figure 15.2). This is accessed by clicking the "Information and Settings" icon (See Figure 15.3). However, be sure to leave e-mail notifications on for the groups whose discussions you are interested in monitoring.

Figure 15.2: You control whether you receive e-mail notifications.

Figure 15.3: Adjust the settings in each LinkedIn group to meet your personal preferences.

Checking out the groups to which your connections belong is the best way to start finding groups. You can also search the Groups Directory using keywords. To do this, click the down arrow to the left of the Search box on the top toolbar and choose "Groups."

As with many other aspects of LinkedIn, successfully using the Groups function comes down to deciding what you want to accomplish on LinkedIn and finding ways to achieve it strategically. Joining these communities is just another way to expand your capabilities and reach on LinkedIn.

APPLYING THE POWER FORMULA

- If you have worked hard at traditional networking, you have undoubtedly been involved with numerous networking groups. These groups have hopefully afforded you a significant number of **unique relationships**, which now will become Number 1 connections on LinkedIn. These same groups may have LinkedIn counterparts that can jumpstart your search for useful connections and increase the power of your searches.

- One of the major benefits of joining groups is your ability to send a direct message to any member of the group. Because your common group membership provides at least a casual connection, this type of message has a potentially higher open-and-read rate than a traditional e-mail to a person you have never met.

Gain direct access to thousands of business professionals with the help of the simple worksheet "LinkedIn Groups: Ca$h in on This Powerful Tool," available on page 205.

CHAPTER 16

Show Me the Money!

What Are the Power Users
Doing on LinkedIn?

I consider power users to be those people who are obtaining significant results in response to their efforts on LinkedIn. The common thread among these successful users is a well-developed strategy and consistent execution of that strategy. Creative and efficient use of the many available features on LinkedIn enables these users to maximize their time spent on LinkedIn and achieve (and in many cases exceed) their specific goals.

I have many opportunities to survey LinkedIn users about the tangible benefits they are receiving from their use of LinkedIn. Though most users can readily report the number of connections they have made through LinkedIn, some are at a loss to identify specific results they have achieved. Inquiry as to their LinkedIn strategy typically results in a response like, "Well, I'm adding lots of connections!" Adding connections without a clear plan can be just as unproductive as physical networking without a strategy for how to meet the right people. Before you spend one more moment on building your network or improving your profile, sit down and document exactly what you are trying to accomplish by using LinkedIn.

Here are some questions to ask yourself as you develop your LinkedIn strategy:

- Can LinkedIn help me find a job?
- Would it be helpful to build a network of people in related industries?
- Can I leverage my relationships with current customers to work toward gaining additional customers?
- Do I want to expand my network of suppliers and gain access to products or services that complement what I sell or provide?
- Can I find new donors and volunteers for my favorite non-profit organization?
- Do I need to hire employees with specific expertise and experiences?
- Could LinkedIn help me become recognized as one of the experts in my industry?
- Can I increase my brand and overall credibility in the marketplace?

This list is not meant to be exhaustive, but it may assist you in identifying potential strategies for achieving measurable results with LinkedIn. I do not believe you should spend time on LinkedIn or any other social media site until you have outlined what you hope to accomplish. Once you have identified your goals, you can identify the strategy that will best help you reach those goals.

The annual survey I conduct, in addition to the countless personal conversations I have with users, enable me to discover how people are using LinkedIn to obtain results. I have used that information to put together a list of the top ten steps you can take to expand your business, add value to your relationships, and improve your overall effectiveness on LinkedIn.

Here they are, David Letterman style, in increasing order of importance. Paul, music please . . .

10. Use the video camera on your smartphone to record individuals at your organization "doing what they do"— including designers, service people, and other employees. Ask them questions about the company and the quality of their work while they are in action, and post the videos in the Professional Portfolio on your LinkedIn profile. You can also use your camera to record customer testimonials about what differentiates you and your company.

9. Before you head out of town for a business meeting, do a keyword search in the area of the country you will be visiting to see if any of your Number 1 connections have contacts there—you may be able to get together with one or more of them to share ideas.

8. Create your own LinkedIn group for members of your industry (or members of a segment of your industry) who live in your region. Set it up as a closed group, one in which you get to control who can join. Once you have established the group, be sure to add value on a consistent basis by sharing helpful articles and links. Consider hosting one or two events each year where members can meet up in person. If possible, make these exclusive events with well-known industry speakers. Establishing yourself as a thought leader in your market should be one of your primary goals on LinkedIn, and leading a vibrant group is a strong step toward that objective.

7. Review "Who's Viewed Your Profile?" frequently. If you find someone who looks interesting, reach out and ask the person how you might be able to help him/her.

6. In the Summary, Experience, and Education sections of your profile, include uploads or links to documents, videos, and websites as part of the Professional Portfolio. Not only does this visually enhance your profile, but the reader can also be directed to a website of your choice to get more information. This makes it easy to impress the viewers of your profile with your expertise, show them your products and services, and move them closer to engagement with you.

5. Set a goal to get an introduction—through LinkedIn or the good old-fashioned way—from one of your Number 1 connections every week. The introduction requests should be the result of strategic advanced searches for your ideal client or customer. Keep in mind that formal introductions via LinkedIn can only be made to second-degree connections.

4. Create a saved search using the keywords that are most important to you, and then LinkedIn will notify you when someone who meets those search criteria enters your extended network. For example, because architects design buildings that will eventually require office furniture, furniture dealers are always interested in forging new

relationships with members of the architectural commu-nity. Therefore, a saved search with the keywords *architect* and *architectural* that targets the applicable geographic market will likely lead to future business opportunities.

3. On a weekly basis, review the first-level connections of your own strategically important first-level connections. My life and disability insurance agent, who happens to be a fra-ternity brother, has consistently done a great job of asking for referrals when we meet for our semiannual breakfast or lunch. Now that I am using LinkedIn, we spend that time talking about our kids and hobbies or reminiscing about the good old days; he can look at my Number 1 connec-tions anytime he chooses. Some people choose to turn off the ability for others to view their Number 1 connections, so you may not be able to do this with everyone in your network. However, the default setting on LinkedIn makes your first-degree connections visible to your network.

As part of your review, use the Advanced Search func-tion to search the networks of your first-level connections (see Figure 16.1). Use the keywords your perfect customers

Figure 16.1: Your friends are ready, willing, and able to introduce you to your perfect targets.

are likely to put in their profiles. If you do this before a meeting or phone call with one of your connections, it's easy to ask your friend for an introduction to the person you'd like to meet—your perfect target!

2. Take a look at the profile of anyone you are meeting for the first time, even if you are just meeting him or her over the phone. This will help you understand that person's business and expertise, and it will enable you to identify common interests and conversation-starters for your initial contact. Most businesspeople are always looking for ways to connect with people on a personal level before jumping into a business discussion. Look for shared connections, groups, skills, etc. on the person's profile (see Figure 16.2). That business professional has put all this information in his profile because he is

Figure 16.2: Do your homework, and add a personal touch to your business conversations.

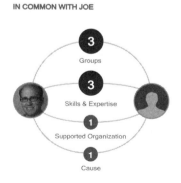

proud of his interests and accomplishments and wants you to know and ask about them. This is a great way to show that you do your homework and care about him as a person—not just as a potential sale.

1. Update your status several times each week using the
   Share an Update box near the top of your home page (see
   Figure 16.3). Much like Twitter, this feature allows you to
   post short updates to your LinkedIn network. Since the

Figure 16.3: Stay top of mind with your network by consistently posting status updates.

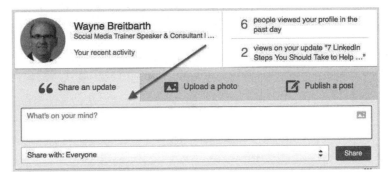

status update does not go out as a message, you do not
need to be concerned about annoying people; the content
you type in this box will only appear in the Top Updates
section of each of your connections' home screens. Some
people choose to receive a weekly e-mail that shows their
network's activity, and those people can also view your
update there.

Status updates are one of the most powerful functions of
LinkedIn. Having your name show up on a consistent basis
on your entire network's home page is invaluable. And if
you're a job seeker, it's absolutely vital. Here are some good
ways to capitalize on this important feature:

- **Share links to interesting articles, websites or
  video.** Don't worry about whether all of your

connections will find the information equally valuable. Use words that grab the readers and encourage them to click the link.

- **Attach a document to your status update.** Your audience might appreciate receiving checklists, white papers, or case studies. Job seekers, this is a great place for your resume.

- **Mention a person or situation that might be helpful to some of your connections.** For instance, "I just met with @John Jones from @ABC Insurance Company and found out they are saving companies lots of $$ on workmen's compensation insurance." The "@" before an individual or company name allows the reader to click through to that person's LinkedIn profile or company page.

- **Talk about an event you are attending or have attended.** This might encourage involvement and/or questions about what you learned there.

- **If you're a job seeker, mention job fairs you are attending, people you are interviewing with, networking events you are going to, etc.** That's more subtle than saying, "Hey, I'm still looking for a job."

Spend some time looking at the status updates of the people in your network to get a feel for what is typically shared here.

After attending my training session for CEOs and learning about the tremendous power of status updates, a local CEO asked his network if they knew any good candidates to fill his vice president of manufacturing position. This resulted in finding a great new executive for his management team and saving $40,000 in recruiting fees.

I have used the status box in a number of ways. When I was involved in the day-to-day operations of my furniture dealership, my service manager informed me on a Friday afternoon that he needed four men for a weeklong project that was beginning in ten days. Since my network is loaded with fifty-year-old people who are always interested in ensuring their college-age sons are gainfully employed, I posted this need in my status update. Forty-five minutes later, I had five strong young men whose parents convinced them they should help me out and pick up some quick cash to pay for a few of their own expenses.

I have used the status box to help my daughter secure a summer job and to assist a nonprofit group in locating tents for an event they were hosting. It would probably have taken several hundred phone calls to get the results I got from simply typing my request into the status box and clicking "Share." However, because LinkedIn is a business site, I would recommend using this tool sparingly for personal requests. Even though many people in your network will be more than willing to help you out both personally and professionally, it's best to not overload their home page with personal requests.

You can also share other people's status updates. Simply click the "Share" on your connection's update, and then select whether you want to share that information with your network, your Twitter followers, specific individuals in the form of a direct message, or selected groups (see Figure 16.4).

You now know ten actions that LinkedIn power users find most useful and effective. Whether you choose to incorporate all

Figure 16.4: If you found a friend's status update to be helpful, your network might appreciate receiving it, too.

ten of them into your LinkedIn strategy or simply focus on the ones that most closely fit your personal networking goals, you will certainly be working toward expanding your business, adding value to your relationships, and improving your overall effectiveness on LinkedIn.

LinkedIn can help you reach more qualified prospects with less marketing dollars. Download "How to Reach Your LinkedIn Audience," available at **www.powerformula.net/audience**, to learn more.

Download "How Does Your LinkedIn Marketing Strategy Measure Up?" available at **www.powerformula.net/marketing**, and use the handy report card to assess the strengths and weaknesses of your strategy.

CHAPTER 17

Your Account, Your Settings— Your Way

Setting Your Preferences and Using the LinkedIn Help Center

You will find that LinkedIn gives you an extensive amount of user control and many resources for solving problems and learning even more about LinkedIn's features.

To access many useful account controls, click "Privacy & Settings," which you will find when you scroll over your photo on the top right of any screen. The Privacy & Settings page is the control panel for everything you can set, turn on/off, and expand on your LinkedIn account. There are numerous settings you may want to explore—many of which are self-explanatory—but I am going to address the ones you will need to understand up front as well as the ones people ask me about most frequently:

- **Public Profile.** In the Profile tab, select "Edit your public profile." This is where you can control which, if any, of the items in your profile will be displayed to those people who are not on LinkedIn but find your public LinkedIn profile as a result of searching your name on the Internet.

- **Receiving Messages.** These settings, found in the Communications tab, allow you to control which types of e-mails you receive from LinkedIn and how often you get them. These e-mails include summaries of your network activity and discussions in groups you belong to. For the most part, your choices are daily, weekly, or never.

- **Viewers of This Profile Also Viewed.** Carefully consider whether you want this box on your profile. If you work for a company, this list will probably include many of your coworkers, which might be a good thing. But I am an independent contractor, and my competitors were being displayed on my profile, which I didn't feel was advantageous. Therefore, I unchecked this box in my profile settings. But even if you choose to remove it from your profile, you will still be able to see this box on other people's profiles.

- **E-mail Addresses.** Be sure to associate all the e-mail addresses you have or have had in the past with your Linked-In account. This setting is found in the Account tab. You may want your primary address (the one to which all of your LinkedIn e-mails come) to be a nonwork address. I have heard horror stories from people who lost their jobs and had a very difficult time getting access to their LinkedIn account.

- **Profile Views.** This setting is found in the Profile tab under the heading "Select what others see when you've viewed their profile." If you want to have your name and headline show up in "Who's Viewed Your Profile?" instead of simply your title and general industry information, change the setting here to "Your name and headline." I recommend this change from the default because it is another opportunity to get your brand in front of LinkedIn members. Think about what we all pay "per touch" in conventional advertising. Here is a freebie!

- **Activity Broadcasts.** You can modify the way others are notified using this setting, found in the Profile tab. The default is that LinkedIn notifies your network every time you make a change to your profile, write a recommendation for one of your connections, or follow companies. I love this, because your name and the fact you made those changes shows up on the home page of every one of your first-level connections. However, if you are spending the weekend working on many changes to your profile, you will want to turn off the notification function either in the Profile tab or with the "Notify your network?" button that appears in the right-hand column when you're editing your profile (see Figure 17.1). Then, after you make the final changes, turn it back on and—presto—LinkedIn tells your network something has changed, and hopefully your connections will take a look at it.

Figure 17.1: When making a lot of profile changes at one time, wait until after you're done to notify your network about your updates.

- **Viewing Your Connections.** This setting, "Select who can see your connections," found in the Profile tab, allows you to prohibit your first-level connections from viewing your other first-level connections. This is an all-or-nothing setting; either all your first-level connections can view your entire network or none of them can view it. Personally, I feel LinkedIn is most effective when everyone shares his/her connections. However, without this feature, some professionals will not use LinkedIn because they see their network as a pseudo client/customer list, and thus they wish to keep it confidential. Do I like it when I can't see someone's first-level connections? No. But I certainly respect his/her right to keep them private.

My advice is to click on each of the settings and find out what options are available to you. The settings I have outlined above are the ones I am asked about most often, but you may find others that will be useful for your situation. There are other ways to change some of these settings, but it is easiest to access them from the Privacy & Settings page because they are laid out in dashboard fashion.

Paid vs. Free Accounts

My latest LinkedIn user survey showed 19 percent of respondents have upgraded to one of the paid LinkedIn accounts—up from 15 percent a year ago. More people are discovering specific features that work well for them, and they upgrade because they want more of those goodies. After five years of using a free account, I personally upgraded to a paid account in 2013. To view a chart that outlines the additional features you will receive with the various types of paid accounts, click "Upgrade," which you will find

Figure 17.2: Some LinkedIn users prefer to upgrade to a premium account.

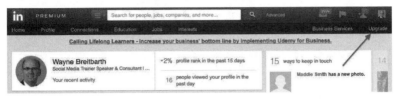

under your photo on the top right of any screen (see Figure 17.2). Consider moving to one of the paid accounts if you are:

1. A human resources professional
2. A recruiter
3. Someone who consistently runs into the screen that says you should upgrade

If you are regularly seeing the screen that suggests you should upgrade, you are probably using a LinkedIn feature that is working for you, and you may want to consider upgrading to one of the paid accounts. For example, if you like to send InMails and/or introductions or would like to have more saved searches, you may want to upgrade your LinkedIn account. In general, I do not recommend moving to a paid account unless you fall into one of the three categories listed above. However, in order to encourage more of us to pay for LinkedIn on a monthly basis, there will undoubtedly be more and more valuable new features available exclusively to premium members.

Features Available to Premium Members
This is certainly not an exhaustive list of LinkedIn's premium features, but here are a few features you might find useful:

1. **More saved searches.** The free account includes three saved searches. Many power users (including me) find this feature to be extremely valuable and well worth the money.

2. **Longer list of search results.** You get up to 100 results on the free account, but a longer list could mean more leads and thus more income.

3. **Who's Viewed Your Profile?** With a free account, you can only see the last five people who have scoped you out. An upgraded account lets you see everyone who's looked at your profile (unless they've blocked their name) in the last 90 days. You can also filter this list by categories like company, geography, and job title, to name a few. This is one of the main reasons I finally broke down and upgraded my account.

4. **Additional advanced search filters.** I especially like being able to filter by company size.

5. **InMails.** An InMail is a direct message you can send to people who are not part of your first-level network. The number of InMails you are allotted per month varies based on the type of premium account you purchase, but you can purchase additional InMails for $10 each. But before buying an InMail, be sure to check if you are in a group with your target, because common group membership enables you to send a free message. Also, if the recipient of your InMail replies within seven days, LinkedIn gives you a $10 credit. The cost of InMails may seem a little steep, but many people find the extra income that results from response to their InMails actually covers the cost of their upgraded account.

Only you can determine whether a premium account will be worth your investment. Personally, I'm happy I upgraded my account, because I've gotten quite a bit of new business by contacting people who have viewed my profile and sending InMails to people outside my network. But if you choose to upgrade and later decide you're not getting as much value as you'd like from your premium account, it's easy to cancel your subscription and return to a free account.

LinkedIn Help Center

Whether you have a free or paid account, LinkedIn has a significant amount of instructional materials available within the site. You can access them by scrolling over your photo on the top toolbar and choosing "Help Center" from the drop-down menu. Simply type your request into the "How can we help you?" box, and you will find a large list of tutorials, including videos, tips, and user guides. The Help Center will be particularly important to you when you are starting out on LinkedIn, but LinkedIn provides extensive information and advice for advanced users as well, and they do a good job of updating these resources frequently.

If you are having specific issues with your LinkedIn account, the Help Center can assist you in resolving them. Enter your question or topic in the Search box. If you do not find an answer to your question, you can contact LinkedIn by clicking "Contact Us." In my experience, the Help Center usually responds within a couple days. And each time I have asked a question, the answer has solved my problem.

Take full advantage of the extensive user controls and helpful resources LinkedIn provides. Adjust the settings to reflect your personal preferences, and you will gain the level of comfort and privacy you desire.

Some people hide their LinkedIn networks, but what's best for you? Discover the answer by downloading "Should You Hide Your LinkedIn Connections?" available at **www.powerformula.net/hideconnections**.

CHAPTER 18

A Job Seeker's New Best Friend

LinkedIn—The World's Largest Internet-Based Resume Database

This chapter is for those of you who are in the process of looking for employment, whether you are seeking to reenter the job market or looking to change or upgrade your current situation. While some of these tips and strategies will overlap with previous chapters, it's important for you to understand the arsenal of tools LinkedIn offers job seekers.

As a job seeker, LinkedIn will be your new best friend because it offers the following valuable capabilities:

- Yours can be one of 400 million "resumes on steroids" employers can search to locate a candidate they would love to hire.
- You can give a vast amount of detail about your skills and experience on your profile, as discussed in Chapter 5.

- You can search for recruiters in any region of the country who specialize in placing people with your expertise.
- You can find out which of your first-, second-, or third-level connections know people at the organization you are targeting.
- If you're currently employed, you can take steps to find a new job without tipping off your current employer.

As I teach LinkedIn training classes, I find that both recruiters and human resources professionals use LinkedIn extensively, many finding themselves checking their account multiple times a day. As a job seeker, that means you should spend a significant amount of your time each day on LinkedIn, networking and optimizing your information to stand out to the people you want to be found by.

For instance, a fellow who attended my training class for job seekers followed my advice and began connecting with employees at a company he was targeting. A few months later, when the perfect position became available at the company, he had an internal fan club waiting to help him. He is thrilled to now have what he refers to as "the job of a lifetime" at the company.

Use the following checklist to help ensure you are availing yourself of the myriad features of LinkedIn that can assist you in finding and securing that next great position:

☐   Be sure your headline states that you are looking for a job. Use very specific language, such as "actively pursuing a job as an IT professional in the fluid power industry" or something of that nature. Your friends want to help you, and your headline should scream out the fact that you are seeking employment and need their help.

☐ Do not list your last job as your current job or people may become confused as to whether you are looking for a job or not. LinkedIn requires you to put a current company name in, which makes this a little tricky; I recommend adding a current job entry like "Sales rep pursuing dealer sales & distribution opportunities," and then put something like "Next Great Company" in the Company Name box. Play around with it and see what you like best. If you are consulting while you seek full-time employment (or if you just list your current job as "Consultant" in an attempt to "look employed"), you may want to say something like "Part-time consultant seeking full-time dealer sales and distribution opportunity." In this case, the words "dealer sales and distribution" should help you move up in the LinkedIn search rankings when people are looking for someone like you.

☐ The first paragraph of your Summary section should explain in a couple of sentences what you consider to be the perfect position for you, and the rest of the detail in your profile should support that. Be certain this paragraph explains to the reader in clear language your goals and your ideal job, so that if he has that job open at his company, he will be able to say, "I just found the person I'm looking for."

☐ Make sure you have at least two recommendations for each job. These recommendations should be specific; they need to differentiate you from the job-seeking masses. As you wait in line for an interview, your profile may be sitting on a human resources professional's desk alongside the profile of the person interviewing directly after you. If you have no recommendations and she has twenty—two or three for each job, in addition to recommendations for her educational entries—who do you think the interviewer will pick? Put yourself in the offensive position, and do not let this happen to you. Go out and get those recommendations. They will serve you well.

☐ Be sure to load your profile with the keywords recruiters will be looking for—terms relating to specific software, processes, degrees, specialties, and training, as well as any other words and phrases that speak to your credibility and education.

☐ Include in your Professional Portfolio items such as your resume, your portfolio, and articles you have written. Consider including a slide show that outlines your career. You may also want to post a video resume on YouTube and put it in your portfolio or link to it through the Websites section of your profile. Video resumes are a very effective tool, and making one is quite simple with the help of your smartphone. A video resume shows your personality, your story, your passion—and the fact that you are technologically savvy.

☐ In your Skills section, it's important to include the skills you hope to utilize in your new job. If you reorder your entries and put these essential skills near the top of the list, people will be more likely to endorse you for those skills. Of course, actively seeking endorsements for those skills will also be beneficial.

☐ When considering the best information to include in your Projects section, focus on projects that will be important to your future employer. You can also impress them and differentiate yourself from other candidates by adding special sections to your profile, such as Languages, Test Scores, Publications, Courses, and Patents. And if you've received honors and awards, don't forget to flaunt them.

☐ If you have attended seminars or received specific industry-related training—especially if the knowledge you gained might be meaningful to your future employer—include this information in your Education section. Describe it in detail and include lots of keywords.

☐ Join groups that are specific to your industry and region of the world. Once you join these groups, it's important to get involved in general discussions, look for job postings and job discussions, and find fellow members who might be able to lead you to your next job. Groups are a simple way to virtually hang out with people who work for companies in industries and geographic regions you have interest in.

☐ To search for jobs that are posted directly on LinkedIn, click the Jobs tab on the top toolbar and type job titles, keywords or company names in the Search box. This will take you to the Advanced Search screen, where you can further refine your search. You can save ten job searches.

☐ One of the major benefits of the Jobs feature on LinkedIn is that when your search brings up a job you're interested in, LinkedIn displays a list of people in your network who work for that company (see Figure 18.1).

Figure 18.1: Someone in your network may be able to help you get the job.

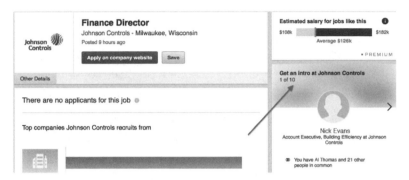

☐ After you have applied for a job in whatever way the application requires (mail, fax, online, etc.), use Advanced People Search to see if you can locate somebody in your network at the first, second, or third level who works for the company or, better yet, is involved in the Human Resources Department or the department you've applied to. Contacting this person may enable you to get your resume to the top of the stack. By effectively leveraging your network, you can greatly increase your chances of getting that job. Remember, your network would love to help you.

☐ You will find it very helpful to look at the LinkedIn company page of any companies you are targeting. Look at the employee list to see if there is anyone who might be able to give you the inside scoop on the position you applied for, the hiring process, the company's political climate. Use the "Follow company" option to keep tabs on the organization on an ongoing basis. I've had people tell me that the HR person at a company they were following contacted them for a position. There is no limit to the number of companies you can follow—so get going.

☐ Be sure to update your LinkedIn status periodically (two to three times per week) to remind your network you are still looking for a job. For example, stating in an update that you will be attending a job fair will not only put your name in front of your network but will also remind your contacts that you need their help in finding a job. Your network will undoubtedly lead you to your next job as long as you keep yourself top of mind among your connections. The Status box is a great way to do that.

☐ In each group there is a Jobs tab that lists employment opportunities and discussions relevant to that community (see Figure 18.2). If, for example, you are looking for a job as a project manager in the construction business, you will want to join groups related to

Figure 18.2: Judiciously joining and being active in groups may be your ticket to the perfect job.

the construction industry and frequently check the Jobs tabs for new postings. Joining fifty groups on LinkedIn will give you access to fifty job boards. Take advantage of this opportunity.

☐ Once you secure an interview, review the profile of the person with whom you will be interviewing and look for areas of common interest you can use as discussion starters. You may find it helpful to look over the recommendations the interviewer has written for others; this will tell you what qualities she appreciates in her business associates. Emphasizing the fact that you possess these traits could prove helpful in securing the position.

☐ An experienced recruiter can be very beneficial in finding employment opportunities, and you can find many good recruiters on LinkedIn. An Advanced People Search will help you zero in on the best recruiters for your circumstance.

If you find yourself in official or unofficial job-seeking mode, LinkedIn should be on your computer screen for several hours each day. You will want to follow the suggestions listed here as well as keeping track of who's meeting whom on LinkedIn and strategizing about how you can engage in conversations with people who can help you find your next job.

APPLYING THE POWER FORMULA

- The person who has the most **unique experiences**, along with the most **unique relationships**, will generally find employment more quickly than other job seekers, especially if he has leveraged the full power of LinkedIn.

- When in job-seeking mode, be careful not to rely solely on virtual tools like LinkedIn and forget that you need to create or reestablish **unique relationships** on a face-to-face basis, too.

CHAPTER 19

Ready . . . Set . . . Go!

A Six-Week, Two-Hour-per-Week Road Map to Results

If you are a novice user or have just now decided to take the leap and begin using LinkedIn, I would like to give you a road map for moving forward and executing a LinkedIn strategy. By spending about two hours per week for the next six weeks, you will be able to execute many of the techniques I have presented. You will find and connect with people you know and trust, and the effort you put into creating a beefy profile will increase the likelihood of your being found. Follow this six-week game plan to make sure you cover all your bases and get off to a strong start.

If you are the owner of or a leader within a company, this game plan might also be a valuable tool for you to use. Some of these steps can be delegated to people who have social media expertise and the time to accumulate and draft the information you are going to include in your profile. However, an important point to remember when you are using LinkedIn—or any other social media tool, for that matter—is that you should always personally communicate with your network.

For example, if you are going to delegate a portion of the responsibility for your LinkedIn profile, such as writing portions of the Summary section or adding connections from a card file, be certain your own personality comes through and you understand the steps being taken on your behalf. This way, you will avoid having someone come up to you and thank you for connecting on LinkedIn when you have no idea who the person is because one of your assistants added him.

Below I have outlined a six-week road map that will assist you in harnessing the power of LinkedIn. This plan should be extremely valuable if you are just beginning your use of LinkedIn. If you already have a comprehensive profile and a documented LinkedIn strategy, you can use this as a checklist to assure yourself that you are on the right track.

Week 1

- Join LinkedIn.
- Accept any invitations that meet your acceptance criteria.
- Put your most recent jobs into the Experience section of your profile.
- Complete the Education section of your profile.
- Invite at least 20 trusted professionals into your network.
- Add a professional-looking high-definition photo to your profile.

Week 2

- Accept any invitations that meet your acceptance criteria.
- Invite at least 20 more trusted professionals into your network.
- Complete the Experience section of your profile.
- Put your company website on your profile, and give it a description other than the standard "My Company."
- Write a killer 120-word marketing headline that includes important keywords.
- Join five groups. Think industry groups, alumni associations, chambers, and large regional networking groups.

Week 3

- Accept any invitations that meet your acceptance criteria.
- Review the "People You May Know" section and send invitations to anyone you know and trust.
- Invite at least 20 more trusted professionals into your network.
- Request a recommendation from a trusted professional who knows you well enough to write a detailed, keyword-filled testimonial about you.
- Write a recommendation for someone in your network who would really appreciate the props.
- Perform a company search on either a competitor or a target organization and "follow" that company.
- Perform an Advanced People Search using the most important keywords for your business or industry in the region you serve. See if you know anyone who comes up in the search results. Send invitations to those who meet your criteria.

- Join five more groups.
- Post a status update that is helpful and/or shows expertise.
- Review "Who's Viewed Your Profile?" and look for interesting people. Send a connection request to anyone you'd like to add to your network.

Week 4

- Accept any invitations that meet your acceptance criteria.
- Invite at least 20 more trusted professionals into your network.
- Add two more items to your Website section.
- Add any significant volunteer work to your current Experience section or Volunteer Experience & Causes section.
- Add any specialty classes or technical industry training to your Education section.
- Write a recommendation for someone in your network.
- Join five more groups.
- Perform a company search on either a competitor or a target organization and "follow" that company.
- Perform an Advanced People Search with important keywords, and send invitations to those who meet your criteria.
- Request a recommendation from a professional you know and trust.
- Using a word processing program, create the text for your 2000-character Summary section. Spell-check it and post it on your profile.
- Post a status update that is helpful and/or shows expertise.

Week 5

- Accept any invitations that meet your acceptance criteria.
- Invite at least 20 more trusted professionals into your network.
- Write a recommendation for someone in your network.
- Join five more groups.
- Perform three keyword searches in Advanced People Search and save them.
- Request a recommendation from a trusted professional.
- Add the Skills section to your profile, and include up to fifty specific skills.
- Connect with classmates using the Alumni Feature.
- Post a status update that is helpful and/or shows expertise.
- Review "Who's Viewed Your Profile?" and look for interesting people. Send a connection request to anyone you'd like to add to your network.

Week 6

- Accept any invitations that meet your acceptance criteria.
- Invite at least 20 more trusted professionals into your network.
- Write a recommendation for someone in your network.
- Join five more groups.
- Find a helpful PDF, video, or presentation and upload it or link it to your Professional Portfolio.
- Ask for an introduction from one of your connections using the LinkedIn Introduction feature.

- Post three status updates that are helpful and/or show expertise.
- Document your specific LinkedIn goals for the next quarter.

Once you have completed this six-week game plan, your compelling profile (including enthusiastic recommendations) and significant number of connections will allow you to consistently be found by people who are searching on LinkedIn. Your use of the search function will enable you to continually find new connections and locate valuable information. And joining groups and getting involved in group discussions will help you continue to expand your presence on LinkedIn.

As you make updates to your profile and more thoroughly develop your LinkedIn strategy, remember that effective networking begins with sharing your knowledge and resources with others. So you should periodically add helpful documents to your profile, and use frequent status updates to share interesting articles, websites, and other information with your network. In the networking world, nice guys finish first!

Managing Your Time on LinkedIn

Just like clockwork, toward the end of each of my LinkedIn classes, someone brings up the issue of time management. The questions typically include:

- How much time should I spend on LinkedIn?
- What should I do with that time?
- How do I make my time on LinkedIn productive?
- How can I be sure I am being productive and achieving my goals?

I have found that the most effective way to manage the amount of time spent on LinkedIn is to follow daily, weekly, and monthly to-do lists. You can expect all of these tasks to take a total of about one to two hours each week, but spending even more time can result in greater value. Trust me—your time investment in LinkedIn will pay dividends. The following to-do lists will help you reach the highest level of effectiveness while keeping the time you spend on LinkedIn at a manageable level.

Daily LinkedIn To Do's

- Review your home page.
- Respond to any messages in your inbox.
- Respond to any invitations to join other people's networks.
- Review the Updates section of your home page to check for interesting events, projects, or comments.
- Check discussions in your two or three most important industry groups.
- Invite people you met the previous day to join your network, as long as they are people you know and trust or you are going to make sure you get together with them to discuss each other's goals and objectives.
- Post a status update. Because updates with links have a much higher chance of being viewed and read, include a link to a helpful article, blog post, or website. If your update doesn't have a corresponding link, include a link to your website.

Weekly LinkedIn To Do's

- Look at new groups your connections are joining.
- Review profile updates of the most important people in your network. To find these, scroll over the down arrow to the right of the gray Endorse button and select "View recent

activity." If you see updates that others in your network might find useful, share, "like," or comment on the update.

- Review the new connections of your first-level connections.
- Look at the complete networks of any new first-level connections who have relevant networks.
- Review the results of your three saved searches.
- Share any relevant articles, blog posts, or events as a discussion in your most important groups.

Monthly LinkedIn To Do's

- Review your profile for possible additions or changes.
- Review your list of first-level connections and identify people you should contact in the near future.
- Consider revising any of your three saved searches for increased effectiveness.
- Review the profiles of several of your competitors. If you don't want them to know you checked them out, go to your setting titled "Select what others see when you've viewed their profile" and select "Totally anonymous."
- Go through your connections list and write two unsolicited recommendations.
- Make a list of people who may derive real benefit from being connected to each other and set up a lunch or breakfast to introduce them.

Periodic To Do's (Every few months)

- Review individual and company profiles of your closest competitors.
- Save and print the latest copy of your profile. You can do this by clicking "Save to PDF" (see Figure 19.1).
- Request an archive of your LinkedIn data. If you click "Request an archive of your data" (see Figure 19.2), you can

Figure 19.1: Save your LinkedIn profile—better safe than sorry.

Figure 19.2: Spend a few minutes saving your LinkedIn data—it's time well spent.

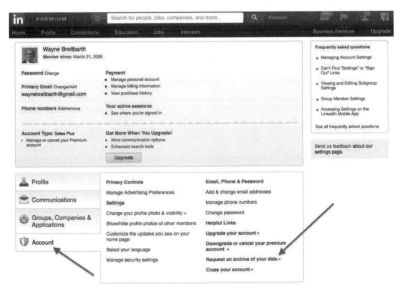

get a zip file from LinkedIn that includes several spread-sheets, including a list of your first-degree connections, the recommendations and endorsements you've received, your search history, and lots more.

You will definitely want to save and print your profile and request an account data download as a safety precaution; I have heard a few stories about data being lost on the LinkedIn site. This is not a common occurrence, but taking the time to safeguard this information is well worth the effort.

Regularly maintaining and monitoring your LinkedIn presence will be instrumental in helping you to meet and exceed your professional goals—whether that be advancing your personal brand, selling your goods and services, or finding a job. And remember—all this can be done while lounging on your living room sofa and keeping an eye on your favorite TV program. Who says it's only the young people who can multitask!

CHAPTER 20

Conclusion (Or Is It Just the Beginning?)
Which Camp Are You In?

You did it. You got to the final chapter of what is probably your first book about the new world of social media. I am honored that you spent those hours listening to me, a 57-year-old businessman, share business experiences I've had over the years. I hope you will apply them to this state-of-the-art tool and improve and expand your marketing and branding efforts.

When I teach my LinkedIn training class for beginners, my goal is to get rid of the fear factor, and as I mentioned in the introductory chapter, that was my goal with this book as well. I truly hope I have allayed any fear you may have had about LinkedIn. I also stated in the introduction that upon finishing this book, you would end up in one of three camps. Let's revisit those three options before you get on with your marketing and branding efforts:

Camp Number 1: "Nah, nothin' here. I understand the tool and its capabilities. It might be good for others, but it's not really for me." At least you now know what your competitors may be doing. Tell your friends and associates who want to connect with you on LinkedIn that you have decided to do your marketing and branding in other ways that you feel more closely fit your skill set and your schedule.

Camp Number 2: "I am going to put LinkedIn on the back burner and possibly use one or two features." If you are in the second camp, you can continue your investigation into LinkedIn by doing one or more of the following:

- Ask some of your trusted friends and associates who spend time on LinkedIn, "What are you specifically doing on LinkedIn and what results have you seen as a result of your efforts?"
- Attend a workshop presented by an experienced LinkedIn trainer.
- Be on the lookout for specific examples and evidence of ways LinkedIn may help you achieve some of your marketing and branding goals.
- Consider bringing in a marketing intern for the summer or for a semester to do a thorough investigation into your competition's LinkedIn presence and activity.
- If you are involved in industry associations or peer groups, suggest that the topic of LinkedIn be presented and debated for the good of all members. You will not be alone in wanting to talk about LinkedIn—I promise!

Camp Number 3: "I get it, I can do this, and I want to do this!" The majority of the people I encounter land in this camp. If you fall here too, you see significant benefits of planning and executing a LinkedIn strategy—and possibly strategies for other social media tools as well. However, you may still be hesitant to make the commitment because you have a busy life and are not sure you want to have to stay on top of another inbox when you could be pursuing your favorite leisure activity. This is where the rubber meets the road. This is where attitude and commitment have to kick in. If you are going to embrace LinkedIn and the changes it will bring to how you do business, you need to believe you will receive real value as a result of the time and effort you devote to developing a presence on LinkedIn.

From my firsthand experience and the reports I have received from people who have embraced LinkedIn, measurable results are typically obtained within two to three months of signing up. Your commitment will pay off, but, as with any kind of networking, patience and diligence are required. Just keep in mind that LinkedIn allows you to grow your network exponentially, and every new connection you make puts you closer to closing that million-cubicle deal.

As your network grows, it is important to continue developing your professional relationships, and sharing your knowledge about the extraordinary capabilities of LinkedIn is one way to do so. Share your success stories with friends and business associates, and show them how to use the LinkedIn features you have found to be most useful—or give them a copy of this book!

Throughout this book I have discussed the Power Formula and what it means to you as a business professional. Remember, your **unique experience** plus your **unique relationships** plus this **tool** (LinkedIn) equals the **power** to execute your business plan at the highest level. LinkedIn may be the newest and shiniest tool in your toolbox, but it can only be effective if you combine it with **what** you already know and **who** you already know. So start connecting today!

My Kids Are Already on Facebook—Can't They Find a Job There?

Why College Students Need to Be on LinkedIn

As the father of three extraordinary daughters, I have experienced the full range of parental emotions—from the highs of birth, first steps, and scoring that first soccer goal, to the lows of the first car accident and less-than-stellar boyfriend. But the top-of-the-mountain moment was the phone call I received from my oldest daughter: "I got a full-time job, Dad, with benefits!"

If you are the parent of an unemployed or soon-to-be college graduate or have a friend who would like to get a kid on his or her way to financial independence, this chapter is for you. As a matter of fact, high school students can now join LinkedIn, too, and it's a great place to find a summer job.

LinkedIn can be quite beneficial when searching for an internship or permanent position, and it can help young people build a solid "professional personal brand." This is the term I use to describe a person's brand in the business marketplace; it is about the person him- or herself and should not be confused with a company's brand or with personal brands on sites like Facebook, which may not be very professional.

Not so many years ago, the phrase "personal branding" was not even part of our professional language, but these days most people realize they need a personal brand in order to succeed. What changed? First, people are not staying in jobs as long as they did when my father and grandfather were in the workforce. In those days, you stayed with a company for a long, long time, and your personal brand was directly tied to the company for which you worked. It had little to do with you as an individual. Nowadays, the average worker holds many more positions throughout his or her adult life, and one job does not define a career.

Second, technology has allowed people to have a very extensive virtual presence, which can impact what they are trying to accomplish in the business world both positively and negatively. Young people are joining social networking sites at the ages of ten, eleven, and twelve years old, but many of these kids fail to recognize how their actions, discussions, and other information they post can negatively affect their future personal and professional brands. On the other hand, these social networking tools, if used responsibly, can play a very positive role in developing a strong personal brand.

Here are the top ten reasons young people should be on LinkedIn prior to graduating from college:

1. They are already on Facebook and other social networking sites, so they will grasp LinkedIn more quickly than people

in my age group. Because the sites operate so similarly, it will not be hard for college students to trade some of their Facebook time for LinkedIn time in order to advance their professional presence in social media.

2. LinkedIn is perhaps the only social networking site a young person's future employer is actually active on. If business executives choose only one social networking site, they typically choose LinkedIn—so young job seekers definitely want to make sure they have a profile there. To assist potential employers in finding him, remind the young person to include his LinkedIn public profile URL on his resume, cover letters, and e-mail signature.

3. LinkedIn users can review and print the profile of the person with whom they are going to interview prior to calling or meeting her. This is an invaluable resource in helping interviewees understand who the interviewer is and finding areas of potential discussion and commonality for their upcoming interview. Remind the young person that the businessperson who wrote that profile is proud of every bit of information included in it. Understanding and remembering it will result in a much richer conversation during the interview, which should give him a competitive advantage over the other candidates for the job.

4. Encourage the young person to prepare a video resume, and have her upload it or place a link to it in her Professional Portfolio or the Website section of her LinkedIn profile. Video resumes are a powerful differentiator for college students, because not only can they go into more detail about their specific accomplishments, but they can also show their personality and passion for their current projects and future goals.

5. LinkedIn allows students to make connections in college that will give their upcoming job search a huge boost. They may say, *Yeah, but I don't know anybody in business, so how can I really go about putting together that muskie net you talked about?* Encourage them to connect with their fellow students, and remind them that the idea is not just to add more Level 1 connections but also the 2's and 3's to which those Level 1's are connected. The minute a student connects with her roommate, she could be adding all the business executives her roommate's parents know into her network. College students should also be connecting with friends of their parents or family members who are tied into the business community. That will allow them to begin having conversations with more seasoned professionals about what the student hopes to accomplish as he or she approaches graduation. Adding fellow students and family friends in the business community is one way to begin a successful business networking career.

6. Students can use LinkedIn to search for internships. Chances are the company he or she wants to get an upcoming summer internship with is on LinkedIn. The student may be fortunate enough to find the specific person he wants to meet, but, if not, he may at least find people in the same department. He can then figure out if someone he knows is connected to those people. Most internships are found through networking, not through answering ads, and LinkedIn can give young people a head start on the networking they need to do in order to find that perfect internship. Students can also use the LinkedIn Jobs function to search for internships.

7. When a student begins her formal job search in earnest, LinkedIn will allow her to look for the people she wants to sit down with to discuss the kind of job she is looking for and how she might go about getting it. These people will function as career mentors to her, and she will have a lot more opportunities to find the right mentors if she is connected to the right people on LinkedIn.

8. LinkedIn can help students put together a target list of employers they may want to work for by using the Field of Study Explorer feature. Access this by selecting "Education" on the top toolbar and then choosing "Field of Study Explorer." Students can then select their major from LinkedIn's list or type their major in the "Browse by name" search box (see Figure BC.1).

Figure BC.1: LinkedIn helps students find employment opportunities and connect with people who can help them get hired.

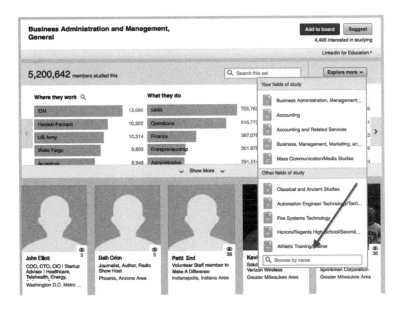

Once they've landed on the page for their major, LinkedIn will display all the people on LinkedIn who have selected that major. They can then filter by:

- Where they work
- What they do
- Where they went to university
- Where they live
- How you are connected

With just a few clicks, students can see what companies in a given city hire people with their major, and they can even see which employees at those companies went to the same university they attend. This is a great place to start when putting together a list of potential employers. Thanks, LinkedIn!

9. LinkedIn can be used as the student's home page or personal website. It can bring together all of the social networking sites he uses (his blog and his accounts with Twitter, Facebook, Google+, Pinterest, etc.). However, he will want to be certain the information posted on these other sites is in line with the professional image he wants to portray. His future employer does not want to hear about his experience hosting parties with beer bongs and bikinis; that type of information can ruin his chances at a job.

10. Special profile sections entitled Courses, Honors & Awards, Organizations, Projects, and Test Scores are particularly helpful for students. In addition, the Volunteer Experience & Causes section allows students to list all of their volunteer work, college leadership experiences, and committees on which they served. This will help to differentiate them

from students who have been less active while attending college. When the student is looking for a job immediately following her graduation from college, she probably won't have a lot of formal job experience; these leadership positions and volunteer opportunities set her apart in the eyes of potential employers. Remember, she gets 2,000 characters for each job and educational entry on her profile. If the student has had these types of experiences, remind her to take full advantage of the Experience section as a way to exhibit her worth to potential employers or individuals who could assist her in her job search.

As valuable as LinkedIn and other social media tools can be in achieving personal and professional goals, they can be equally detrimental if a person's online presence is inconsistent with his or her actual personality and character. College is the best time to begin thinking about who you are, what you stand for, and what type of company you wish to affiliate yourself with, and LinkedIn can get students started towards that positive, powerful, "professional personal brand" that will stick with them throughout their career.

APPLYING THE POWER FORMULA

- Even though the young person in your life may be just beginning his professional career, he already has **unique experiences** that could be very helpful to him in his upcoming job search. Internships, organizational involvement (especially leadership positions), and summer employment can be explained on his LinkedIn profile in such a way that they will show prospective employers that the student is the type of strong candidate they are looking for.

- Employers aren't the only ones who can write recommendations. Leaders of organizations, teachers, and professors can also help students substantiate some of the **unique experiences** they have had through a testimonial on LinkedIn.

- The special profile sections and Professional Porfolio feature discussed in this book can help students more effectively convey their collegiate experience in ways that will differentiate them from other candidates. Understanding and using these tools could significantly enhance the student's ability to tell the story of his or her **unique experience**. Plus, proficiency on LinkedIn is a skill many employers will regard as leading edge.

- Students' **unique relationships** with teachers, parents, mentors, and other students can lead to second- or third-degree connections that may help them land that important interview.

FOR MORE INFORMATION . . .

VISIT www.powerformula.net to:
- Receive notices of updates to this book
- Download free resources
- Subscribe to Wayne's weekly LinkedIn tips
- View video clips
- Purchase a LinkedIn training course
- See what others are saying about *The Power Formula for LinkedIn Success*

FOLLOW Wayne on Twitter at twitter.com/WayneBreitbarth for daily LinkedIn tips.

JOIN the conversation by becoming a member of the Power Formula LinkedIn group.

CONTACT Wayne at wayne@powerformula.net or visit his website to learn more about the valuable services he provides, including:

- Corporate consulting and training
- Keynote and breakout presentations for conventions, conferences, and corporate events. See Wayne's energetic and humorous presentation style at www.youtube.com/user/wbreitbarth.

Resources

It's All About Character
Take Full Advantage of Every Space

There are limits to how much information you can include in each section of your LinkedIn profile. Here is a handy list of the character limits for each field.

Note: The numbers in parentheses represent the maximum characters allowed. This means letters, spaces, and punctuation marks—*not* the number of words.

Individual Profile

Headline (120) This is the most important real estate on your profile. Include the keywords people typically use when searching for someone in your space. Tell your story. Impress your target audience.

Summary (2,000) It's like a cover letter—or your 30-second elevator pitch. *Here's how I can help you.* Tell your story. And don't forget those keywords!

Specialties (500) LinkedIn appears to be phasing out this section of the profile and has added the Skills section instead. If you are lucky enough to have a Specialties section, including lots of keywords here will obviously cause more people to find you when they are searching on LinkedIn.

Website Descriptions (30) Be sure to use all three slots and describe them accordingly.

Experience Title (100) Go beyond your standard biz card title. Be creative with keywords.

Experience Description (2,000) You can mention your past experience, but focus more on demonstrating your capabilities. Describe not only what you *are* doing but also what you *can* do to help customers/clients. Include keywords, of course.

Education/Degree (100) Rather than simply putting BBA, MBA, etc., add descriptive phrases that might help people discover your profile when they do a search; for example, BBA with an international accounting emphasis or BBA with a minor in Spanish.

Education/Fields of Study (100) Highlight classes you took that relate to what you are doing in your current position or the position you are seeking.

Education/Activities and Societies (500) Be descriptive. If you were the president of Beta Alpha Psi, the viewer of your profile will recognize your leadership ability. If you were the captain of the field hockey team, a kindred spirit may reach out to you.

Interests (1,000) You may want to show just a bit of your personal side but not too much. It's not Facebook, after all.

Organizations (1,000) This is a good place to share organizations that may or may not have their own official LinkedIn group.

Honors & Awards (1,000) If you don't toot your own horn, nobody will. Be proud. These entries are important differentiators and build credibility.

Skills (80) You can list up to 50 skills, and you have 80 characters to describe each skill. So don't shortchange yourself. This is great for SEO of your profile.

Advice for Contacting (2,000) In addition to your business e-mail address and phone number, you may find it beneficial to include the types of inquiries you're interested in receiving.

Phone number (25) If you choose to list your phone number, only your first-level connections will be able to see it.

Address (1,000) If you include your address, it will only be visible to your first-level connections.

Other Limits

Company name (100) If your company name is less than 100 characters, I suggest adding a few of your most important keywords here.

Direct, first-level connections (30,000) Believe it or not, some people actually reach their limit.

Outbound invitations (3,000) You can request more, and LinkedIn seems to give them out pretty freely at 100 per request.

Maximum number of groups (50) But this doesn't include subgroups. You know the drill here. The more groups you're in, the more people you can find and the more who can find you. There are over two million groups. I'm sure you can find 50.

Status updates per day (no limit) I suggest doing a couple each day.

Number of characters allowed in status updates (600) However, only 140 will transfer over to Twitter.

I hope you're encouraged to take full advantage of these LinkedIn limits.

Profile Perfection
A Checklist for LinkedIn Optimization

This handy checklist will help you develop a dynamic profile that will increase your visibility, set you apart from your competition, and quickly attract your target audience.

Your most important keywords (KW)

1. _____

2. _____

3. _____

4. _____

Note: Consider placing these keywords in some or all of the sections with the (KW) designation.

You will be much more effective if you complete the basic profile sections.

- ☐ Name

- ☐ Headline (120 characters max) (KW)

- ☐ Photo

- ☐ Experience (Include a detailed job title and job description with keywords, if possible, and your company's standard descriptive language) (KW)

- ☐ Location and industry

- ☐ Education (college, high school, specialty schools/ courses)

- ☐ Contact information

- ☐ Public profile URL (as close to your name as possible; e.g., www.linkedin.com/in/waynebreitbarth)

- ☐ Summary (Include your company's standard descriptive language) (KW)

- ☐ Websites (List three and describe them)
  - Your company website
  - Other company website page (company video, mailing list sign-up, etc.)
  - Website of personal interest (favorite charity, college attended, etc.)

Set yourself apart by strategically including additional profile sections.

- ☐ Professional Portfolio
  - Audio
  - Videos
  - PDFs
    - ○ White papers
    - ○ Research documents
    - ○ Case studies
  - PowerPoints
  - Photos

- ☐ Volunteer Experience & Causes

- ☐ Certifications (KW)

- ☐ Languages

- ☐ Patents

- ☐ Publications (KW)

- ☐ Skills & Endorsements (Include up to 50 skills) (KW)

- ☐ Courses (KW)

- ☐ Honors & Awards

- ☐ Organizations

- ☐ Projects (KW)

- ☐ Test Scores

Take these additional steps to more fully optimize your profile.

☐ Connections (More is better, but carefully develop a connection strategy that's right for you)

☐ Recommendations (Try to get at least two for every job and education entry) (KW)

☐ Groups (Join up to 50 groups—more is better, but choose them strategically)

☐ Status Updates (Show your network you're a thought leader by sharing interesting and helpful information)

☐ Endorsements (Seek them for your most important skills)

LinkedIn's Websites Section
Your "Link" to Future Opportunities

The websites section is a simple but powerful way to generate not only interest and increased credibility but also business leads. Encourage people to click the links by strategically using the available 30 characters to describe each of your three websites.

What kind of links should I include?

Choose websites, videos, blogs, etc., that will inform, encourage, or help others. Here are a few ideas for using these important links.

☐ **The home page of your company website.** Of course, this should be first. Change the description from "My Company" to something more descriptive, like your company name or tagline.

☐ **The mailing list sign-up page on your company website.** This is a good way to build your database.

☐ **Articles, customer testimonials, case studies, white papers, or other documents that are on your company website.** The LinkedIn profile is all about showing your expertise. These are great ways to showcase your accomplishments.

☐ **The sign-up page for an upcoming company-sponsored event.** This is a terrific way to increase attendance at your event.

☐ **Videos you've posted on your company website, on other websites, or on YouTube that show products, presentations, testimonials, etc.** Video is really hot and getting hotter, and making one is simple with the help of your smartphone. People love seeing and hearing other people.

☐ **Links to either a completed survey of industry matters or an ongoing survey for which you need more opinions.** People love data and being a part of the data group.

☐ **A specific call to action.** "Request a quote" or "Get more information" are great ways to encourage the reader to contact you.

☐ **Websites of related organizations, associations, industry groups.** You can show your involvement and at the same time promote the group.

☐ **Your blog.** If you are writing content that is important to some or all of your LinkedIn audience, this is really a power tool in your journey to be the most credible person in your space.

☐ **Special promotions or giveaways.** People love free stuff and will be very willing to click the link.

☐ **Your Facebook, Pinterest, or other social media accounts.** These are great as long as the content on these sites will not jeopardize your professional credibility. It is not necessary to include your Twitter account in the Websites section. There's a separate spot for that just below this section.

☐ **The website of your favorite charitable organization.** This shows people what you are interested in and at the same time helps promote a group you really care about.

LinkedIn People Searching
Your Ticket to Improved ROI

If you don't begin with a specific strategy to find the right people, you'll waste a lot of time searching on LinkedIn.

This worksheet will help you decide which people you want to meet. To help you get started, I've included examples of keywords I've used to locate prospects for my office furniture business. The profiles of people in your network who hold positions similar to those of the people you want to meet are great places to look for the keywords your prospects might be using.

On the lines below, jot down the keywords you'd like to use. Try arranging them in different combinations. Then use the Advanced Search function to begin searching for people who have included these words in their profiles. Because you can direct-message anyone in your LinkedIn groups, that is another great place to use these words and search for the people you want to meet.

Stop wasting time. Develop a sound strategy for finding the right people, and watch your ROI soar.

Titles used (Facilities Manager, Facilities Director, Facilities Planner, VP-Facilities)

_____

_____

_____

_____

Category (customer, referral partner, etc.)

_____

_____

_____

_____

Keywords that describe them (purchasing, procurement, buyer, project management)

_____

_____

_____

_____

LinkedIn defined industry (facilities services)

_____

_____

_____

_____

Geographic region (Milwaukee, Wisconsin)

_____

_____

_____

_____

LinkedIn groups they belong to (IFMA, BOMA, Corporate Real Estate & Facilities Management Professionals)

_____

_____

_____

_____

Specific strategic action steps to meet the right people; include time frame for accomplishment (I will join and be active in one new facilities-related group in the upcoming year.)

_____

_____

_____

_____

Keywords

The Key to Being Found on LinkedIn

Be sure your most important keywords are used numerous times in your profile. Note that keywords in starred sections carry extra weight in the LinkedIn search algorithm. The places you should include your keywords are:

- ★ Headline
- ★ Experience: job titles
- ★ Skills
- • Summary
- • Experience: description of jobs
- • Recommendations
- • Interests
- • Courses
- • Projects
- • Publications
- • Certifications

As you complete the worksheet below, it will be helpful to include different words people may use to describe the same thing, like *attorney* and *lawyer, legal* and *law, editor* and *proofreader, teacher* and *instructor.*

Titles you hold or have held

_____

_____

_____

_____

Job responsibilities you have had

_____

_____

_____

_____

Types of products or services you sell

_____

_____

_____

_____

Brand names of the products you sell

_____

_____

_____

_____

Brand names of the services you sell

_____

_____

_____

_____

Specialty certifications or degrees you have received

_____

_____

_____

_____

Industry-specific courses you have taken

_____

_____

_____

_____

Names of software you can use proficiently

_____

_____

_____

_____

Regions of the world you specialize in serving

_____

_____

_____

_____

Your present and past employers (including any corporate name changes)

_____

_____

_____

_____

Clubs, associations and groups to which you have belonged

_____

_____

_____

_____

Hobbies/activities you want your business connections to know about

_____

_____

_____

_____

LinkedIn Groups
Ca$h in on This Powerful Tool

You can join up to 50 groups on LinkedIn, and I suggest you take full advantage of all this potential. By joining groups, you increase the size of the population you have access to when doing any type of search. Once you find members of the group who meet your search criteria, you can communicate with those people even though they may not be connected to you at the first, second, or third level.

Get started by filling in the blanks below with words that describe you, your business, and your target audience. To jump-start your thought process, I've included examples of keywords I used to locate prospects when I was in the office furniture business.

After you complete this worksheet, click the down arrow next to the Search box on the top of any LinkedIn page and select "Groups." Enter the keywords you've jotted down below in different combinations. You'll find lots of great groups you can join to achieve your business goals.

Geographic region or area you serve and/or where your suppliers or customers are located (Midwest, Wisconsin, Milwaukee)

_____

_____

_____

_____

Industries you sell to or receive supplies from (education, real estate, flooring)

_____

_____

_____

_____

Professional interest or areas of expertise (accounting, interior design, sustainability)

_____

_____

_____

_____

Products/services you sell (office furniture, carpeting, interior design)

_____

_____

_____

_____

Your customers and vendors (architect, facilities manager, moving company)

_____

_____

_____

_____

People who also serve your customer base (real estate developer, general contractor, architect)

_____

_____

_____

_____

Professional titles of your customers or suppliers (president, flooring distributor, CFO)

_____

_____

_____

_____

Clubs or associations you belong to (AICPA, ACG, Waukesha Chamber, Marquette Alumni)

_____

_____

_____

_____

Your hobbies and interests (hiking, scuba diving, fishing, social media, classic rock music)

_____

_____

_____

_____

Acknowledgments

What a wild ride it has been—writing a social media book at age fifty-three, watching it become the number-one-selling Linked-In book on Amazon.com, and now publishing a third edition. I couldn't have done it without the help of the following people:

Brenda (my wife, best friend, grammar czar)—You have been the inspiration for the book in so many ways—from your beginning declaration, "We should write a book," to your many, many hours of typing, proofing, editing, convincing, and, most importantly, persevering. You're great!

Erica, Jenna, and Deanna (my daughters and personal consultants for "all things computer," graphic design, and Facebook generation philosophy)—Simply put, you guys rock!

Wayne and Marge Breitbarth (my parents)—Even though you will never be on LinkedIn and perhaps never read more than this page of my book, your living examples of what it means to be a friend, business owner, and parent have had an immeasurable influence on the experiences and perspectives that I share throughout the book. I love you!

Tim Rudd (my good friend and former partner)—Thanks for being the most understanding partner a guy could have during my exploration of LinkedIn.

Bob Hetzel (my faithful friend)—Your constant encouragement, whether hiking in Colorado or making business and life decisions, always motivates me to get to the top.

Todd Schwerm (my good friend and first LinkedIn connection)—Without your persistence in telling me "You've gotta join LinkedIn," I would not be writing this book. Thanks for caring so much about me.

Joe Guidi (Mini Me)—Your youthful insights about how younger business professionals think and act have helped me every step of the way. You are wise beyond your years (and an awesome son-in-law, too).

Jack Covert (business book author and founder of 800-CEO-READ)—Without your taking my phone call ("Wayne who?"), spending time talking about my book, and ultimately recommending Greenleaf Book Group, the final product would not be what it is. Thanks also for helping businesspeople across the country know what business books to spend our precious time on.

The Team at Greenleaf Book Group (my publisher)—Thanks to all of you for sharing your expertise and skills and for having the patience to answer my many questions. Clint, you have put together a team of real professionals who care.

Jason Alba—Your book *I'm on LinkedIn—Now What???* started me down this path. I don't know whether to curse you or hug you, so I will stick with the latter. Thanks for being a pioneer.

Jan Vermeiren—Your book *How to REALLY Use LinkedIn* helped me get to the aha moment of realizing you'd better have a strategy on all this social media stuff or not waste your time.

Neal Schaffer—Your book *Windmill Networking: Understanding, Leveraging & Maximizing LinkedIn* and your blog posts are my continuing source of "go deep" information on everything LinkedIn.

Gary Vaynerchuk—As I am writing this with my "Crush It" wristband on, I am thankful for the inspiration your book and videos have given me to do just that—crush it.

Erik Qualman—Your book *Socialnomics* was the first book I read that connected the dots for me on how social media works from a 35,000-feet view. Thanks also for your video "Social Media Revolution," which is a powerful closer for many of my social media presentations.

David Meerman Scott—Had I not devoured *The New Rules of Marketing and PR*, I would not have come to the realization that we are all thought leaders at something, and the Internet is our way to be able to create a "worldwide rave."

My Early Audiences (my guinea pigs)—I can't believe you had any interest in listening to a CPA/office furniture guy talk to you about something you wanted nothing to do with and then told your friends to do the same. I couldn't have and wouldn't have wanted to do this without your encouragement.

Pepsi Max (my caffeine elixir)—I don't know that I could have gotten through all the writing and editing without the extra caffeine and ginseng with which you are so lovingly loaded.

Jesus (my Lord and Savior)—Your example of how to connect with people is the standard for which we should all strive.

Index

About the Author

 Wayne Breitbarth is a nationally recognized LinkedIn speaker, author, and consultant. The first edition of his book *The Power Formula for LinkedIn Success* was the bestselling LinkedIn book on Amazon for more than a year and a half. Wayne has helped more than 80,000 people maximize their use of LinkedIn. He has inspired audiences both locally, at many of Milwaukee's most prominent companies and organizations, and nationally, at conventions, industry association events, and corporate training sessions. Wayne's diverse business experience, pragmatic teaching style, and infectious sense of humor have earned him the praise of the press and the distinction of being referred to as the "LinkedIn Guru."

When he began using LinkedIn in 2008, he was an owner and president of M&M Office Interiors in Pewaukee, Wisconsin. He currently devotes himself full time to helping companies develop a comprehensive strategy for using LinkedIn to increase sales, raise brand awareness, recruit employees and reduce recruiting fees, and discover new markets for products/services. In addition, he helps individuals maximize their use of LinkedIn to meet and exceed their professional goals and advance their careers.

Prior to his involvement in the office furniture business, he spent nearly twenty years in the automotive industry. He received his BBA from the University of Wisconsin-Whitewater and his MBA from Marquette University. Wayne is also a Certified Public Accountant and spent the early years of his career as an auditor and small business consultant with Arthur Andersen & Co.

Throughout his career, Wayne has been involved with a number of philanthropic organizations. His financial background has enabled him to assist Make A Difference-Wisconsin in its mission to enrich the community by empowering high school students to make sound financial decisions. His work with this organization includes serving on its board of directors as well as teaching financial literacy classes to students in Milwaukee Public Schools. He is also the founder of Urban Promise, an urban youth mentoring program that brings together business professionals and high school students in Milwaukee Public Schools. Wayne also serves on the board of directors of the Community Warehouse, a nonprofit organization that serves the Milwaukee community by providing affordable home-improvement materials, and Milwaukee Working, a nonprofit in the Central City that creates jobs for men and women who are either underemployed, never employed, or background challenged. He has also served as a youth leader and teacher at Eastbrook Church in Milwaukee.

Wayne's work with urban youth has been applauded by the Wisconsin Institute of Certified Public Accountants, and he is a past recipient of the WICPA Public Service Award.

Wayne resides in Milwaukee, Wisconsin, with his wife of 35 years. They have three daughters and one granddaughter.